STRESS FREE
in 30 DAYS

STRESS FREE
in 30 DAYS

Charles Linden
Creator of **The Linden Method®**

HAY HOUSE

Carlsbad, California • New York City • London • Sydney
Johannesburg • Vancouver • Hong Kong • New Delhi

First published and distributed in the United Kingdom by:
Hay House UK Ltd, Astley House, 33 Notting Hill Gate, London W11 3JQ
Tel: +44 (0)20 3675 2450; Fax: +44 (0)20 3675 2451
www.hayhouse.co.uk

Published and distributed in the United States of America by:
Hay House Inc., PO Box 5100, Carlsbad, CA 92018-5100
Tel: (1) 760 431 7695 or (800) 654 5126
Fax: (1) 760 431 6948 or (800) 650 5115
www.hayhouse.com

Published and distributed in Australia by:
Hay House Australia Ltd, 18/36 Ralph St, Alexandria NSW 2015
Tel: (61) 2 9669 4299; Fax: (61) 2 9669 4144
www.hayhouse.com.au

Published and distributed in the Republic of South Africa by:
Hay House SA (Pty) Ltd, PO Box 990, Witkoppen 2068
Tel/Fax: (27) 11 467 8904
www.hayhouse.co.za

Published and distributed in India by:
Hay House Publishers India, Muskaan Complex, Plot No.3, B-2,
Vasant Kunj, New Delhi 110 070
Tel: (91) 11 4176 1620; Fax: (91) 11 4176 1630
www.hayhouse.co.in

Distributed in Canada by:
Raincoast, 9050 Shaughnessy St, Vancouver BC V6P 6E5
Tel: (1) 604 323 7100; Fax: (1) 604 323 2600

Text © Charles Linden, 2013

The moral rights of the author have been asserted.

The information given in this book should not be treated as a substitute for
professional medical advice; always consult a medical practitioner. Any use of
information in this book is at the reader's discretion and risk. Neither the author
nor the publisher can be held responsible for any loss, claim, or damage arising
out of the use, or misuse, of the suggestions made, the failure to take medical
advice, or for any material on third party websites.

A catalogue record for this book is available from the British Library.

ISBN: 978-1-78180-153-6

Previously published in 2007 by LifeWise Publishing (ISBN: 978-0955656804)

Printed and bound in Great Britain by TJ International, Padstow, Cornwall.

*Dedicated to Charlie and Florence, and my
grandma, Kathleen Florence Lampitt (1911–2005)*

CONTENTS

CONTENTS

FOREWORD

We all experience work and life pressure at some point during our lives, and while some people thrive on these times, others can eventually fall to pieces physically and emotionally. Staying together in stressful times isn't about physical or mental strength; it is partly to do with emotional intelligence, but mostly to do with perception.

While one person might perceive their situation as dire, another might perceive that same situation as exciting or challenging, while others might find it as dull as ditchwater.

We are all different, all the product of our individual environments, our experiences, and our genetics. However, while genetics play a definite role in determining our familiar predispositions to certain traits or conditions, the environments we experience as we go through life have the most dramatic influence on how we react emotionally and physically in any given situation.

in the form of retreats and workshops. These are visited by people from every corner of the world, including industrialists, actors, sportspeople, celebrities of every type, and hundreds of people just like you and me.

> 'I had been very ill during and after a recent pregnancy, and had terrible anxiety and nervousness as a result of the illness, even though I was slowly getting better. I met Charles, went on the retreat, and started following his method immediately. It really worked, and now I am doing all the things that I used to do before I stopped. I started riding again, working, going out and about, driving, taking the train etc. – all the things that make life fun, but which I had felt unable to do.'
>
> *Plum Sykes, Vogue USA fashion editor*
> *and bestselling novelist*

What we achieve is unique, and curatively more effective than anything else available. The collective knowledge and experience of the team means we 'leave no stone unturned' when someone asks for help. We are proud of the respect, referrals, and support we receive from medical practitioners, psychologists, academics, and clients from around the world; people who call The Linden Method 'a new branch of psychological practice' that works. To me, it's just the program that has changed my life in many beautiful ways.

Much of what we have learned while developing The Linden Method to help high-anxiety sufferers has also proved the answer for helping many people beat stress and take control of their lives again. If you follow the recommendations made in this book, you will eliminate stress and worry from your life. However, you need to be READY to make some changes in your life practices: the way you think and the way that you behave.

This is a one-size-fits-all program designed to bring balance to your physical and mental self. It is time and user tested, distilled from the most relevant information we've gathered over our many years of research, and delivered to you in an easy-to-use and potent format.

Stress can have far-reaching and invasive consequences. Sufferers often experience anxiety disorders, phobias, panic attacks, or depressive thoughts, but with a slight alteration in perception, stress and all of the symptoms it brings with it can be eliminated or avoided completely.

Charles Linden

 # Introduction

YOUR FIRST STEP TO RECOVERY STARTS HERE

Congratulations on taking your first step toward eliminating stress and worry from your life… permanently!

I guarantee that by following the guidelines and suggestions in this book, you WILL SEE RESULTS in less than 30 days. And if you continue using the guidelines and tips you receive throughout this 'boot camp,' you will be able to manage your stress and worry much more effectively, because you'll understand the key secrets of creating lasting balance in the bodily systems that control how you feel. This program is a 30-day plan but, hopefully, most of what you learn you will take with you for the rest of your life.

During the next 30 days I'll make recommendations about changing your diet and lifestyle, and how you perceive your environment. The stress-busting methods contained in this book are based on the testimonials of the many people we have helped, and I have used many of them to release myself from stress and anxiety. Whether you choose to follow my recommendations is entirely your decision.

Ready to make some changes?

I know everyone wants a 'magic pill,' a 'quick-fix' remedy – swallowed in seconds and with immediate results. Unfortunately, this simply doesn't exist. Stress and worry are behaviorally based; they result from your inability to cope successfully with life pressures.

But over the next 30 days, you'll learn how to change all of that. Using the tips and techniques in this book can help you to eliminate the physical symptoms of stress by rebalancing your bodily systems, creating balance in your daily routines, and STOPPING worry in its path.

> 'I realized I had been feeding my anxiety, when what I needed to do was train my brain to steer away from it.'
>
> *Jemma Kidd, international make-up artist and columnist*

This program recognizes that everyone is different physically and emotionally, as well as having very different routines, goals, and ambitions, but this is irrelevant. By implementing structure in every element of your life, you can quickly eliminate those things that cause you most emotional and physical harm – it's all about balance and perception. Balance in the body and mind, and your perception of your situation. If you feel overwhelmed by work for example, chances are that you're not managing your time efficiently. The only way to combat this is to implement behavioral 'tactics' to create balance and change your perception of the situation at hand. You either see it as a stressor or a challenge – it's your choice. BUT one produces positive change, the other perpetuates negativity.

Becoming stress free in 30 days is implemented by following the instructions you receive daily. I can't force you to do the things I suggest; you may even feel that they are futile. However, trust me, having helped tens of thousands of people worldwide, our research is pretty conclusive. The structure I'll suggest to you can and will bring about many positive changes; permanent ones that will create a solid foundation on which to build the challenges, dreams, and achievements of your life to come.

> 'Life is now something I can look forward to, not fear. Working in the charity sector as a director and founder around mental health, I can say that if peace is what you are looking for, look no further.'
>
> *Rupert Young, charity director, brother of Will Young,*
> *the international artist and* Pop Idol *winner*

Some days the instructions might be quite simple to implement, on others they may be more difficult, but please try to comply with them as closely as possible. Some days the instructions may not be relevant to you; if that is the case, don't do them… it's that simple.

Throughout the book you'll find recommendations for supportive resources that we've tried and tested over the years and which have proved to be of value to our clients. The accompanying audio CD contains some powerful visualization tracks that you may find helpful during the next 30 days, and beyond.

You are now well prepared to commence the journey into the rest of your life – stress, anxiety, and worry free. I suggest you start to read and implement my advice immediately.

WHAT IS STRESS?

First of all, let's discover the kinds of things that cause stress. Stress can be due to anything that creates an imbalance in your practical and emotional life. This could be bereavement, work pressure, financial worries, health concerns, bullying, or any number of issues that might be insignificant to others, but which nevertheless impact your 'life practices' (the way you want to live your life) and/or emotions.

Stress is the negative manifestation of life pressure. This can be due to any one of the examples mentioned above, but these are not stress, they are the normal and expected issues of life. However, we all react differently, and our tolerance of such issues differs massively from one person to another. What is one person's passion could be another person's poison: base-jumping doesn't fill me with exhilaration, but for many people it's a walk in the park! Some people seem to thrive on challenges that increase their anxiety levels, while many people develop anxiety disorders, panic attacks, or other behavioral conditions when experiencing similar levels of physical and emotional stress.

Please don't think that this is a sign of weakness; many stress and anxiety sufferers find themselves suffering precisely because they are so strong – the weaker people tend to drop out of the race early on, due to a kind of 'self-preservation' response that prevents them from pushing themselves too far. Stress and anxiety sufferers tend to be strong and able, intelligent and driven.

Stress in controlled doses can be good for us, but when the stress is relentless, it no longer drives ambition but produces unpleasant and sometimes very frightening physical and psychological symptoms.

It isn't uncommon for people to become 'stress chasers.' Like storm chasers, these people look for trouble and thrive on the challenges of overcoming it. Similarly, many recovered stress and anxiety sufferers develop an attitude of 'I've been to hell and back and now I have tamed the monster, I am going to exploit it!'

What are the physical manifestations of stress?

Initially, the most obvious physical manifestations during periods of stress are chemical. In the brain, hormonal changes in the hypothalamus cause reactions in the pituitary gland, which in turn causes the adrenal glands to release adrenalin (epinephrine) into the bloodstream.

Adrenalin is the hormone that regulates the anxiety response, often called the 'fight-or-flight response.' This response is activated in times of real danger that require us to either fight or run from that threat in order to survive. When this mechanism developed in the human body, it was designed to prepare it to go into combat with fierce animals for example, or, if combat was futile, to run away.

It has been some time since saber-toothed tigers roamed the land, and so the anxiety response has become more useful for coping with near crashes, bar brawls, stressful emails, work deadlines, and other such wonders of modern life.

The problem is, the human body hasn't had time to adjust or evolve to distinguish the differences between prehistoric and modern life, so the anxiety response is still very unrefined, and sometimes highly inappropriate. It is especially inappropriate when it reacts under circumstances such as life or work stress, where the extreme fight-or-flight response is overkill.

Environmental stimuli from the sensory organs collect information about the potential threat and feed those signals back to the brain, specifically the hippocampus and the amygdala. This should, under 'normal,' appropriate circumstances, provide the brain with enough information to enable it to react appropriately to the situation at hand – but it doesn't always work out that way.

When stressful life circumstances repeatedly produce this type of reaction, and regularly raise the anxiety and stress levels **above** your normal, preset levels, changes happen in the amygdala that cause it to become **stuck** at a much higher level of reaction. The **benchmark level** of stress or anxiety that triggers this response is lowered, meaning the sufferer becomes **more reactive under much less threatening circumstances**.

The brain is like a computer – it stores and releases information – but with one important difference. A computer stores information in file systems, but brain learning happens through building new file systems called 'neural pathways.' Neural pathways build constantly in the brain; they are the building blocks of memory, physical and mental response, and learning. As the anxious habit forms, the brain quickly builds new neural pathways for this new behavior and labels them as NORMAL.

When we feel anxious or stressed as a result of these changes, we know that they are wrong, but the brain thinks they are completely normal.

Stress and anxiety breed stress and anxiety

As we experience escalating stress and anxiety, we become weakened emotionally and physically, and very soon, a cycle of fear and stress can become the 'norm.'

To a certain extent, our physical makeup and genetics dictate how we react during these times, and it is said that some people have a genetic predisposition to such problems. However, I believe that **environment** and **emotional intelligence** are primarily responsible for stress and anxiety conditions, and this theory is strongly reinforced by the clients who have used The Linden Method to overcome such issues. But let me explain how these two factors affect stress levels:

⊙ **Environment:** Your environment is anything that is external to you, including your work, home, and social settings. Your environment is anything that exists beyond the surface of your skin.

- **Emotional intelligence:** This is the kind of intelligence that makes people capable of invention, creativity, and problem solving. It doesn't necessarily manifest as artistic, musical, or literary creativity – it can be the ability to problem solve or think outside the box.

Of course, it is important to understand that some people may not have access to the level of support that others have. Some sufferers are alone with their condition, either due to a lack of family support or a lack of emotional attachment to those who might otherwise help them through such difficult times.

Our ability to interact with others can have a knock-on effect throughout our family, work, and social experiences, and can heavily influence our reaction to stressors and anxiety-provoking situations. This can also have quite a profound effect on our self-image and self-confidence, which in turn can affect our social behaviors, alcohol consumption, diet, drug use, and many other factors.

Psychological development

Throughout the twists, turns, highs, and lows that life presents, we adapt and learn from each and every experience. Some people cope and adapt better than others, and this can be due to previous life experience, and whether they have adopted the negative or positive behaviors or guidance from others – e.g. parents and other family members, peers, teachers, and mentors.

It is vital to understand that, regardless of whether or not you have a genetic predisposition to stress-related conditions, the reason you are suffering right now is purely dependent on your **perception** of the situations that have given rise to the initial stress: e.g. work pressures, bereavement, relationships, financial worries, etc.

More often than not, people with a predisposition to developing stress conditions automatically focus on the worst-case scenario, the ultimate catastrophic outcome, and in doing so they embellish the situation's true nature and often miss the simple solutions. How you see your situation, regardless of whether you are seeing it accurately or inaccurately, is irrelevant. What is important is that **you change your perception by training your mind to react more appropriately to stressors**. Stress is not an illness - it can be eliminated, and so can all the physical conditions caused by it, such as generalized anxiety, panic attacks, OCD, phobias, and all the physical sensations, disturbed thoughts, or emotions you may be experiencing.

The good news is that by using a structured stress elimination program, some common sense behavior modifications, knowledge, and reassurance, you can and will be stress free once again.

Remember: understanding stress

- ⊙ *Stress is the physical manifestation of pressure or stressors.*
- ⊙ *Stress can create changes in the body that can feel frightening and unpleasant.*
- ⊙ *Stress is the brain's learned response to negative behaviors and thoughts, and perceived danger.*
- ⊙ *Some people thrive on stress – others don't.*
- ⊙ *You will be stress free once again, because stress is a transient state; it is all about changing your perception.*

Stress levels and response

The level or type of stress experience not only affects one person more radically than the next, but can also cause very different physical and mental manifestations. How an individual experiences life events is usually dependent on what else is going on in their life at the same time, e.g. with their health, job, or relationship. A combination of badly timed events create a reaction that would not happen at other times.

The ratio of 'stressful event' to 'ability to cope' fluctuates throughout our lives, and sometimes it takes something as simple as a common head cold to knock us sideways and cause a cascade of bad fortune, stress, and emotion. Our reaction to an event is vital to the impact that it has on our lives, and so it is important to understand that by modifying the way we respond, we can change its impact on us!

When confronted by a potential stressor, we make a decision on how to react based on what we perceive through our sensory organs. Subconsciously we may experience an uncontrollable anxiety response and experience the familiar symptoms of fear, BUT our conscious reaction to that stressor can be controlled. Some people allow their subconscious mind to lead them to a decision; others are more measured and controlled, and so make a more intelligent decision before responding.

At this point, having high levels of emotional intelligence is a disadvantage, because it is those people who generally suffer the most. Unfortunately for stress sufferers, those who respond more appropriately at these times are those who generally have a lower emotional response to everything in life. Patience and self-control are key here, even when it goes against your normal behavior to be that way.

Making the decision about how to react is what I describe as a 'binary decision.' Binary is the digital language used by computers, and it works like a mathematical on/off switch. This is because computers calculate by asking questions: is the answer a one or a zero? If it's a one then it switches one way; if it's a zero, it switches the other.

Having a head cold puts you into a binary state – you either have a cold or you don't; it's either a one or a zero. So, how you respond consciously to anything is a binary decision – you can either take route one or route zero. You see there is a formula that is followed by the brain when confronted by a stressful event, as the following diagram illustrates:

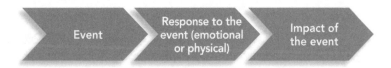

So depending on how you **perceive** the impact of an event depends on how you **react and manage** the outcome of that event and how you then cope with any consequences of that event.

For example, a loss of income to someone with children, a mortgage and car payments would be catastrophic, whereas to a single person living at home and driving dad's car when they need it, the consequences of a job loss would be emotional but, nonetheless, a lot less significant.

But why should it be? A loss of income could be perceived as a massive blow, or as an opportunity to take on new challenges or a career change. The whole experience may appear impossible or catastrophic at first, but with careful management, structure, and thought, it could be a blessing in disguise – it's all down to perception. Fear is built from catastrophic thought processor thoughts of 'What if…', and these thoughts fuel anxiety disorders.

The fear of consequences can be overwhelming, causing some people to develop extreme behaviors such as agoraphobia or social phobia. These issues are actually a very effective method of self-preservation, because they prevent the sufferer from having to face whatever they perceive as a threat in the outside world. However, this self-preservation cocoon is incredibly detrimental, as they experience high levels of anxiety and maybe even panic attacks when they try to leave it. This anxiety is caused by what I call 'false fear,' which is a fear of something that hasn't or may never happen.

🦋 Remember: response to stress

- ◉ *Stress levels are a direct response to your ability to deal with whatever demands are placed on you.*

- ◉ *The conscious part of that process is based on making binary decisions – you either decide to cope or you don't.*

- ◉ *Stress can lead to the development of other physical and mental conditions if not dealt with correctly.*

Common stressors

Although there are many, many reasons for stress, too many to list, there are a number of life circumstances that most people would cite as the source of their stress. These include:

- Divorce
- Moving home
- Bereavement
- Pregnancy or hormone issues
- Job loss
- Lifestyle change
- Relocating to another area or country
- Work stress
- Children starting school
- Money worries
- Relationship problems
- Illness
- Abuse
- Diet
- Child leaving home
- Bullying

Some people may experience a number of these issues throughout their lifetime, others may never experience any, but it seems certain that the more driven and dynamic you are, and the more success you experience in life, the more of these stressors you'll experience. Some are events of everyday life that can't be avoided, others are born of indecision, or are issues that require you to walk away from certain situations; all are open to interpretation and can be overcome in a wide variety of ways.

ALL of these issues can be controlled in order to minimize their effect on your wellbeing, IF you know what to do.

Understanding your stress

You may be able to identify the original event or source of your current stress. The problem with this, however, is that in attempting to use hindsight to identify the catalyst for your present stress, you may apportion blame to a blameless experience. This is a dangerous practice.

Many people give blame to people or situations and later discover they were not to blame at all. It is also common for stress sufferers to apportion blame to what they identify as the catalyst (e.g. relationship problems or bereavement), only to discover that the catalyst was much earlier and they've wrongly identified something else, often something also caused by the catalyst.

For example, a friend always thought her stress and anxiety started as a result of her divorce, whereas in fact the relationship broke down *due to* her stress and anxiety, and started much earlier, after the death of her father. It is so easy to be wrong, so it is much better to move forward instead of trying to place blame. Hindsight is a great thing, but if the catalyst for your anxiety has been and gone, it is pointless to dwell on it.

It is vital that you only apportion blame to CURRENT situations, IF you are certain that these are the reason for your current high stress and/or anxiety. The here and now is the most important. Why? Because the things you can manipulate, change, affect, or improve at this moment in time are the ones that can truly help you to recover for the future.

The events with the most impact tend to be:

◉ Those that happen out of the blue
◉ Those that you have not experienced before.

It is to these types of event that people react inappropriately. These inappropriate responses are physical, emotional, and cognitive (behavioral). It is all too easy to allow these responses to negatively impact our lives, and let the turmoil take over logic and spiral seriously out of control.

Create a life map

An important exercise we do with all our clients to help them find the source of their stress and/or anxiety is to create a life map.

A life map can be created using a sheet of blank paper and a pencil. Starting at the top center of the page, create a flow chart of all the things that you can remember that have impacted your life. It is vital to think of both positive and negative experiences. Try to date them if possible, and place them in chronological order, starting at your birth and ending at the present day. Include events such as dietary changes, smoking start or cessation, illnesses, house moves, birth of children, etc.

By doing this simple exercise, you'll be able to build a clearer view of everything you have experienced during your life, and identify patterns of behavior or catalysts for stress. Stress often follows definite patterns in some people's lives. Many recently retired people find that stress started as a result of a change in routine and a lack of activity. Some young people identify partying too hard, drinking, smoking too much or taking drugs as the catalysts.

Also try to identify any conflicts you have experienced, or are still experiencing. These could be at work, at home, with parents, or siblings. It could be that another person is negatively affecting your self-esteem, or that you're feeling stifled by your relationship, your job, or even your children. It could be that you have general anxiety about life and your place in it.

The warning bells

As a reaction to stress, you may have developed anxiety, panic attacks, insomnia, or phobias. You might experience migraine headaches, a bad temper, or mood swings, for example. Everyone reacts differently, but only you know your body, how to read the signs, and what seems unfamiliar.

The initial stages of stress usually manifest as changes in mood, behavior, or emotions. Ask your partner or close family members whether they've noticed any changes. The people closest to you are usually a good gauge of changes in you that have gone unnoticed by you.

Anxiety, irritability, and moodiness are all emotional responses to stress and result from reaching a point where you feel less or unable to cope effectively. Be mindful of how you react to otherwise fairly moderate stressors. Some people also react to stress with dietary changes: some eat more, some eat less, some binge, and some starve themselves. A depleted diet will only add to your body's stress levels.

So, if you find yourself snapping at others inappropriately, or if you're not eating correctly, take a long hard look at what the sources of these changes might be; consider them carefully and make a plan to reverse them sensibly, while dealing directly with the stress itself.

Many people compensate for their low mood by drinking alcohol or smoking. You don't need me to tell you that this is neither a solution nor sensible. Both substances are stimulants that can only make you feel worse and carry no therapeutic value whatsoever. Although you may feel mildly better afterward, it's short lived and damaging to your long-term recovery.

Here is a list of some of the more common emotional responses to stress. While long, there may be some experiences that are not listed:

- Anxiety
- Panic
- Phobias
- Obsessions
- Moodiness
- Aggression
- Sadness
- Indecisiveness
- Social phobia
- Guilt

- ◉ Tension

- ◉ Boredom

- ◉ Lethargy

- ◉ Tiredness

- ◉ Insomnia

- ◉ Sudden crying

- ◉ Fear of death

- ◉ Agoraphobia (fear of being alone or away from a place or person that offers security)

It is vital that you address any stress issues immediately and identify stress as the cause of these emotions and symptoms.

Don't sit back and think that, given time, things will get better; this is rarely the case. However, you can experience profound improvements by making some very simple changes in your life practices and perception.

Remember: avoid toxic belief systems

Stress breeds fear. Fear is anxiety, and anxiety lives off your concerns, your worries, and your stress. IF you start to believe that there is something else physically or mentally wrong with you, you'll start to build belief systems called 'catastrophic thinking' or 'what if' thoughts. These are the food of anxiety, and once you start down this road of obsessive thinking it is difficult (but not impossible) to pull logic and reason back into line.

Stress can cause a wide variety of strange and sometimes quite frightening bodily sensations and thought patterns, but they are not signs of illness; they are simply the physical manifestations of stress and/or anxiety in the body – they are the sensations of fear. Sometimes these symptoms come on rapidly, and sometimes they can be constant over a number of hours or even days. However, they are transient.

Some symptoms may feel uncomfortable – e.g. chest pains, muscle pains, dizziness, and shaking – but again, these are all normal physical reactions to stress, so please don't fear them.

Also be aware that Googling for answers is not productive; in fact, quite the opposite. The internet and the accessibility to information can be as damaging as it can be helpful. Self-diagnosis is not a viable, reliable, or sensible option. Always seek professional diagnosis; this is vital to your recovery. A medical practitioner will be able to put your mind at rest without subjecting you to millions of alternatives as to what your symptoms *might* be, which is exactly what the internet does – it fuels your fears. A doctor's diagnosis is medical, qualified, and informed, so accept it and then move on with the solution instead of trying to assign blame or popping a pill (the easy option), rather than the little bit of hard work it may take to implement the TRUE solution. There is no 'magic pill.'

So, how does stress affect you physically?

The level of stress experienced by each individual sufferer varies dramatically. Some people react with mild aches and pains, others develop high blood pressure, headaches, palpitations, or panic attacks. Regardless of how stress manifests, the condition can be undermined and eliminated using the same techniques. Here is a list of more common physical stress and anxiety symptoms:

- Chest pains

- Palpitations, rapid heart rate

- Abnormal or fast breathing

- Panic attacks

- Stomach problems (bloating, diarrhea, constipation, butterflies, etc.)

- Muscle aches and pains – back and shoulder pain

- Insomnia

- Muscle tremors or twitches

- Tingling in hands, feet, or limbs

- Strange sensations or tingling in the face, scalp, or neck

- Lethargy, weakness, or shaking

- Dry mouth

- Electric shock feelings in the body

- Eyes feeling like they are staring

- Headaches

- Urgency to urinate or defecate

- Sweating

- Feeling inappropriately hot, or too cold

This list is by no means complete, but it highlights the range of symptoms more commonly experienced. If you have stress, or have been diagnosed with an anxiety disorder, you'll find many of these symptoms very familiar indeed.

If you are under a lot of stress but don't have many, if any, of these symptoms, don't worry that you might develop them, chances are you won't.

When sufferers become aware that stress is the cause of their condition, these physical manifestations commonly stop developing and start to retreat. Stress and anxiety breed in ignorance, but if you recognize the signs, this knowledge tends to halt their development. The fear of the fear and the sensations themselves are what fuel the stress and anxiety; if you take that fear away the conditions retreat.

Remember: to get results, put what you learn into practice

The 30-day program will provide you with many practical ways of minimizing the effects of stress. Please use them, and do not undervalue them. It's all too easy for those who take a grim view to see stress and anxiety as a kind of weakness, and to dismiss some of these techniques as hogwash. However, these may be the very ones that return you to normal. Yoga, Pilates, tai chi, aromatherapy, massage, and other treatments don't just relax you, they also build your self-esteem and confidence, and have enormous value, IF they are relevant and beneficial to you. Let's face it, if someone told you that your stress would disappear if you jump up and down on one leg holding a carrot between your teeth while humming the 1812 Overture, you'll probably do it.

Stress and anxiety elimination isn't rocket science, and the 30-day program is born of many years of careful development, research, and experience in successfully treating clients. If you're asked to do something, it is because it's been shown to be therapeutic to others. Anything that has no, or little, value isn't mentioned.

Behavior that supports stress can cause psychological symptoms

Stress causes behavioral changes in the brain. Each time you change your behavior, your brain busily creates new neural pathways of learning that become concreted into your subconscious. These stay there until superseded by replacement behaviors and newer neural pathways. Neural pathways are constantly being created, modified, and pruned. This physical wiring is pruned away to make way for new neural pathways. The head has finite space in which the brain must fit, so these physical changes allow learning to happen without the need for more space.

Many stressed people become highly dependent on their family, partners, or friends; others withdraw socially, and some develop phobias or belief systems about their condition. Stress and anxiety can cause a variety of psychological symptoms. Here is a list of the more common ones:

- Anxiety and anxious reinforcements through catastrophic thought processes ('what if' thoughts)

- Social withdrawal

- Agoraphobia

- Anger, aggression, frustration

- Feelings of depression, morbid thoughts, or fear of dying

- Feeling like you are losing your mind

- Depersonalization and de-realization – feeling dreamy, or as if your mind has left your body

- OCD – compulsions that result from obsessive thinking, such as contamination issues, tidying, hoarding

- ◉ Weird or disturbed thoughts, sometimes of an aggressive or sexual nature, even against your values or beliefs. This is often referred to as pure O.

All of these inappropriate thoughts are due to and perpetuated by behavior modifications that occurred as a response to increased levels of stress. All of these symptoms are normal reactions to changes in body chemicals and are experienced, to a greater or lesser degree, by almost every stress and anxiety sufferer.

It is vital that you understand that none of these symptoms are a sign that you are losing your mind or are mentally ill in some way. It is also vital to understand that all of these symptoms slip away as you start to tackle your stress and anxiety.

Behavior and our reactions to stress can cause many strange and quite frightening symptoms and, as discussed previously, we are all built differently and react in a wide variety of ways to similar situations.

By behaving like a stressed person, we become stressed as our behavior and our reaction to stress catalysts are what program us to be stressed and for the stress to escalate. By breaking the cycle using behavior modification – while simultaneously changing your perception of the situation and using practical tools to alleviate the stress – a full recovery is possible.

By following the guidelines in the 30-day program – giving structure to your life and work practices, nurturing your body and providing it with what it requires in order to function efficiently, and shifting your perception – you can and will regain control of your life, eliminate stress, and become more effective in every way.

 # Day 1

DIET

How important is your diet to your physical and mental health?

Put it this way, it is the most important factor in your life that you have TOTAL control over in order to maintain physical and mental wellbeing, BUT it is also the most badly executed, poorly managed, widely misunderstood, and massively ignored factor too.

If I told you to put diesel in your gas-guzzling car, would you? You see, diet is that important! By filling your car with the wrong type of fuel you create a massive rejection process that causes the car to splutter and die. Your body is that engine, your food is that fuel, and I can't begin to tell you how VITAL this is!

So many people reject the concept of 'correct diet' as ridiculous, mostly based on comments like, 'I can eat what I want and never gain weight' or 'I've got the constitution of an ox.' These comments might be true to an extent; however, the hidden dangers of food and, more importantly, the hidden effects of food, even when there are no apparent immediate reactions, can have far-reaching health consequences.

🦋 Remember: you need the right fuel

To reject the concept of a good diet is to reject the building blocks of wellbeing itself. In order to gain and maintain physical and emotional balance in which you feel stronger, more alert and able to cope with both the physical and mental exertions of life, it is vital that you maintain a healthy diet. A good diet is a cornerstone of good health and must never be underestimated.

By a healthy diet, I don't mean that you should buy a diet book and stick to it; I mean that you should evaluate what a person of your size requires in sustenance in order to carry out your daily activities, without allowing your body to receive either too much or too little food. Too much of the wrong foods or too little of the right foods, or receiving those foods at the wrong times, can dramatically affect how you feel.

By preventing the seesawing of blood sugar levels, by maintaining healthy levels of vitamins and minerals, and by providing your body with the right fuel in correct quantities at the right times, you can feel much better physically and emotionally very quickly indeed.

A balanced diet is vital for maintaining general good health. Avoiding over-spicy foods, too many carbohydrates, sugary foods, and bad fats is the predictable advice of dieticians the world over, but in the quest for eliminating stress, anxiety, and worry it is vital to maintain an equilibrium throughout the digestive process and throughout the day and night.

So, what should you eat?

Minimize sugar highs caused by foods such as sugary carbohydrates by eating smaller, more regular meals of steamed vegetables, fish, poultry, and fruit. Avoid piles of potatoes, white pasta and rice, bread, cookies and cakes: they produce fast, short-lived sugar highs that can leave you feeling tired and shaky as your blood sugar level drops. The buzzword in any diet is 'balance.'

In addition, there are four main issues concerning diet that are relevant to stress sufferers:

1 Stress can be made worse by a change of diet.

2 Diet can affect levels of anxiety and stress.

3 Stress and anxiety can affect the way the body accepts foods.

4 Sedatives or other medications can make changes in the body, causing food intolerances and other digestive problems.

There is a distinct correlation between a change of diet and the onset and perpetuation of stress and anxiety.

Scientists are beginning to understand a little more about the role of diet in psychological conditions. They have recognized that anorexia may not be totally to do with self-image, and that an element of such conditions is caused by a change in the levels of certain brain chemicals, including histamine, released after eating. These can also manifest as unpleasant symptoms, anxiety, and psychological disturbances, which can cause the sufferer to experience dramatic mood changes, disturbing thoughts, obsessions, and other psychological anomalies. These disorders are caused by the inappropriate thoughts produced by the anxiety response. These, too, like the inappropriate compulsions in OCD (hand washing etc.) and the inappropriate safety-seeking in agoraphobia, are simply an anxious mind's response to 'what if' risk assessments sent out by the anxiety response.

My team and I help people suffering not just from anorexia or bulimia, the two most common eating disorders, but from a wide range of other eating disorders, e.g. the use of insulin to control eating, laxative use, and dietary control in which people restrict what they eat to one food type.

Histamine is a chemical usually associated with allergic reactions; its inappropriate release into the bloodstream can cause unpleasant symptoms including anxiety, palpitations, and other unusual bodily sensations and symptoms.

Scientists have become aware that foods can cause a variety of conditions, and research is being done to isolate those that can be controlled by diet. There is much emphasis on psychological disorders, as these seem to be the worst affected by food intolerances and allergies.

It is thought that even severe disorders, such as schizophrenia and clinical depression, can be treated or controlled by diet. Scientists are currently treating psychiatric disorders with strictly controlled diets and are having remarkable success.

Similarly, stress conditions can be affected by diet; and diet may play a vital role in their development and could dramatically embellish the symptoms experienced if not monitored correctly.

Resources

Scientists in London have found a strong correlation between mental illness and diet, especially a shortage of omega-3 fatty acids (found in oily fish), which affects the levels of serotonin in the brain, causing depression. The rate of depression in New Zealand, for example, is much higher than that in Japan, because the Japanese have a diet rich in oily fish containing fatty acids, whereas the average diet in New Zealand is based on red meats, much like most of the Western world. If you want to read the findings for yourself, you can do so at http://www.sciencedirect.com/science/article/pii/S0165032797001663.

Understanding the effects of food

When I first suffered from anxiety I had changed two aspects of my life; I had given up smoking and was on a strict diet to lose a little weight. I believe that these two factors contributed to the formation of the initial anxiety I experienced.

There is little doubt that blood sugar levels play a distinct role in anxiety. As my anxiety increased, I noticed that certain foods eaten at certain times could drastically affect the way I felt. I soon found that by controlling what I ate I could lessen my symptoms.

This is not a psychosomatic symptom of anxiety; it is quite real and affects many stress and anxiety sufferers to varying degrees. This effect is caused mainly by the disruption of the system that controls insulin production in the pancreas and is called 'hypoglycemia.' Insulin is the chemical that is excreted by the pancreas in order to maintain a healthy blood sugar level.

Many people believe that eating sugary foods will keep them active and stop them from feeling tired, blissfully unaware that, in fact, the opposite is true. As blood sugar levels peak after eating they drop down rapidly as the body uses up the energy created. If you eat very sweet food, the sugar is used up very quickly, causing your blood sugar level to shoot up and then plummet very quickly, and creating the symptoms of hypoglycemia. Coupled with maladjusted production of insulin during stress and anxiety, this combination can leave you feeling very unwell indeed.

Healthy blood sugar levels are vital

When we eat, and food is converted into sugar, insulin released by the pancreas should keep our blood sugar levels constant. When we are stressed, anxious, or in withdrawal from drugs (including alcohol, cigarettes, sleeping pills, antidepressants, and tranquillizers, which can disturb blood sugar levels), the pancreas can produce too little or excessive insulin, causing our blood sugar level to fall or rise to unacceptable levels. This can cause many unpleasant symptoms that can be misdiagnosed as stress conditions such as anxiety, or even depression.

Most sufferers immediately recognize a definite relationship between what they eat and how they feel, and start a game of diet modification that is often misguided and erratic!

You might find that certain foods affect the way you feel; if this is the case, it is advisable to consult a medical practitioner, who may refer you to an immunologist for allergy testing or a dietician who will be able to advise you about a more suitable diet.

During the times when your body is under stress it is common to experience food sensitivities. This is due to alterations in the function of the immune system and can also be worsened by the use of certain drugs prescribed for stress and anxiety, including sedatives and antidepressants.

It is important that you ask for advice about your diet from your medical practitioner or a dietician, but here are a few guidelines for maintaining healthy blood sugar, vitamin, mineral, and fiber levels.

A balanced diet should contain carbohydrates, good fats, proteins, minerals, vitamins, water, and fiber in the right proportions. All of these nutrients are important to maintaining a healthy body. All of the food you eat affects the way you look, feel, and act.

Remember: food provides
- *Energy to move and live a full and active life.*
- *The raw materials your body needs to produce new cells and repair old ones.*
- *The raw materials your body needs to make substances used to control important bodily functions such as hormones, including insulin, adrenalin, and serotonin.*

Healthy eating habits
No one needs to be made more anxious by eating foods or adopting eating habits that do exactly that. Here are five tips that you should make the foundation of your daily eating plan. They will help you to maintain good health, and build a sound foundation for your recovery.

1. Eat complex carbohydrates

Slow-release carbohydrates act as tranquilizers by increasing the amount of serotonin – the neurotransmitter that calms your nervous system – produced by your brain. Eating a diet high in fruit, vegetables, whole grains, and unrefined foods (brown pasta, rice, oats, quinoa, etc.) is helpful for increasing your complex carbohydrate intake. Fruit and vegetables are also loaded with vitamins and minerals and are a great source of fiber.

2. Increase your intake of tryptophan

Tryptophan, a precursor to serotonin, is found in a wide range of foods and has a calming effect on the body. Eat a diet that includes turkey, eggs, soybeans, and milk, all of which contain high levels of tryptophan.

3. Eat more protein

Fish, poultry, meat, eggs, milk, cheese, yogurt, nuts, seeds, pulses, and soybeans contain important amino acids (the body's building blocks) and also provide a range of minerals and vitamins vital for health.

4. Cut down on or avoid refined carbohydrates

White bread, pasta and rice, chocolate, cakes and cookies, fizzy or sweet drinks, and cane sugar are all refined carbohydrates and raise your blood sugar levels. Switch to whole grain, unrefined cereals breads, pasta, and rice, and check food labels for hidden sugars (they are everywhere).

5. Eat more fiber

Fiber plays a very important role in efficient digestion. It is found in fruit, vegetables, pulses, and whole foods. Fiber is not digested in the intestines, and passes through intact, adding bulk to feces and cleansing the digestive tract. If you suffer from constipation or diarrhea, fiber may help to improve your digestion.

6. Eat regularly

Starving yourself and missing meals puts your blood sugar out of whack, so aim for small, frequent meals to maintain your energy levels (without recourse to stimulants such as caffeine) and help to keep blood sugar levels even. Bear in mind that some people can become allergic or sensitive to certain foods during times of anxiety and withdrawal. If you feel that this might be the case, consult your medical practitioner or dietician, who will assist in finding alternative sources of the vitamins and minerals found in the allergy-producing foods.

7. Fats and oils

Contrary to the advice in some 'diet' plans, you do need fats in your diet, but they should be the 'good' fats found in foods such as oily fish, nuts and seeds, and cold-pressed oils (olive, grape seed, etc.), and avocados. These fats are rich in vitamins and minerals, and offer a host of health benefits. Saturated fats, found in animal products, cakes, cookies, pastries, margarines, pre-prepared and fast foods (e.g. palm oil and hydrogenated vegetable oil) are bad fats. In other words, they will make you gain weight and are not digested efficiently. Eat more oily fish (e.g. mackerel), which is rich in omega-3 fatty acids, but avoid fatty meats. Try to avoid eating animal fats and boost your intake of the good vegetable fats.

8. Vitamins

Vitamins are a necessary part of our diet, although only small amounts are required each day. Vitamins are organic substances that act as catalysts in the metabolic processes of the body. Doctors started to recognize that people deficient in certain vitamins became more susceptible to specific illnesses. For example, it was known over 200 years ago that vitamin C deficiency caused scurvy.

There are 13 vitamins known to us, and the top five most important vitamins are A, B, C, D, and E. During times of stress and anxiety deficiencies in vitamins can become apparent, but be aware that is important not to take more than the recommended daily allowance of any vitamin. Multi-vitamins are available from health food shops and pharmacies. Do not take too much extra vitamin C, as my experience and feedback from clients indicates that it can cause you to feel much more anxious.

Here is a list of vitamins, and where they are found naturally in food.

VITAMIN A (RETINOL, BETA CAROTENE)

Sources: Eggs, dairy products, cod liver oil, and vegetables – especially orange and yellow fruits and vegetables, and leafy green vegetables.

Dietary role: Vision, healthy bone growth, and tissue repair.

Deficiency: Night blindness and dry skin conditions.

VITAMIN B1 (THIAMINE)

Sources: Brewer's yeast, milk, oatmeal, brown rice, vegetables, potatoes, liver, and eggs.

Dietary role: Energy, nervous system, muscles, heart, growth, and mental agility.

Deficiency: Depression, moodiness, and nervous disorders (alcohol abuse leads to deficiency in vitamin B1).

VITAMIN B2 (RIBOFLAVIN)

Sources: Liver, dairy products, eggs, vegetables, fortified cereals, and bananas.

Dietary role: Energy, absorbing vitamin B6, and tissue repair.

Deficiency: Lack of energy, skin and eye conditions.

VITAMIN B3 (NIACIN)

Sources: Cereals, whole grains, pulses, vegetables, fish, and mushrooms.

Dietary role: Digestive system, skin, circulation, and energy.

Deficiency: Lack of energy, depression, and skin conditions.

VITAMIN B5 (PANTOTHENIC ACID)

Sources: Liver, eggs, potatoes, cruciferous vegetables, legumes, avocados, and bananas.

Dietary role: Absorption of carbohydrates, lipids, and proteins.

Deficiency: B5 deficiency is extremely rare. It causes fatigue and apathy.

VITAMIN B6 (PYRIDOXINE)

Sources: Eggs, wholemeal bread, fortified cereals, nuts, meat, cruciferous vegetables, and bananas.

Dietary role: Red blood cell production and a healthy immune system.

Deficiency: Anemia, skin conditions, and low energy (depression).

VITAMIN B7 (BIOTIN)

Sources: Raw egg yolk, liver, peanuts, leafy green vegetables.

Dietary role: Cell growth and metabolism.

Deficiency: Digestive problems and skin conditions.

VITAMIN B9 (FOLIC ACID)

Sources: Liver, nuts and seeds, green leafy vegetables, whole grains, fortified cereals, and yeast extract.

Dietary role: Essential for cell division (required pre-conception). Women planning a pregnancy, or in the first 12 weeks of pregnancy, are advised to take a folic acid supplement.

Deficiency: Neural tube defects in babies (if mother deficient), fatigue, sleep problems, and poor mood.

VITAMIN B12 (CYANOCOBALAMINE)

Sources: Fish, meat, dairy products, fortified cereals, yeast and yeast extract.

Dietary role: Red blood cell production and a healthy immune system.

Deficiency: Fatigue, anemia, lowered immune system (strict vegetarians and vegans may need to supplement this vitamin).

VITAMIN C (ASCORBIC ACID)

Sources: Citrus fruits and fresh vegetables.

Dietary role: Absorption of iron, healthy immune system, skin, bones, and teeth.

Deficiency: Lowered immune system, fatigue, and depression.

VITAMIN D (CALCIFEROL)

Sources: Fish, margarine, butter, egg yolks, fortified breakfast cereals, liver, and sunlight.

Dietary role: Absorption of minerals, bone and teeth formation and maintenance.

Deficiency: Bone and muscle weakness (rickets in childhood), depression, and skin problems.

VITAMIN E (TOCOPHEROLS)

Sources: Seeds and nuts, whole grains, cereals, fruit, and leafy green vegetables.

Dietary role: Circulation, cell repair, and healthy skin.

Deficiency: Increased risk of serious disease (e.g. heart disease, cancer).

VITAMIN K (PHYLLOQUINONE)

Sources: Green leafy vegetables, egg yolk, and liver.

Dietary role: Blood clotting and healthy bone growth.

Deficiency: Vitamin K deficiency is rare, and taking additional supplements is not advised or necessary for most people.

CAUTION

You should get dietary advice from your medical practitioner before taking supplements.

9. Minerals

As with vitamins, the body only requires small quantities of minerals. Unlike other dietary substances both vitamins and minerals do not need to be digested; they are absorbed straight into the bloodstream through the stomach lining. Iron is very important in the carriage of oxygen around the bloodstream: it is the mineral used in the production of hemoglobin and is also responsible for the red color of blood. If iron levels are depleted so is the level of hemoglobin in the blood. This causes a lack of oxygen around the body, which in turn causes fatigue. Taking a high-quality multi-mineral supplement is always a good idea.

Here is a list of minerals and their roles in our diet:

BORON

Sources: Fruit, vegetables and nuts.

Dietary role: Proper mineral absorption.

Deficiency: Depressed growth and osteoporosis.

CALCIUM

Sources: Leafy green vegetables, milk, cheese, yoghurt, shellfish, bonemeal, dolomite, almonds, and liver.

Dietary role: Development of healthy, strong bones and teeth; assists blood clotting, nerve transmission and tranquilization, heart rhythm.

Deficiency: Back and leg pains, heart palpitations, tetany, brittle bones, insomnia, tooth decay, and muscle pains.

CESIUM

Sources: Foods grown in mineral-rich soil.

Dietary role: Energy, brain function, and cancer prevention.

Deficiency: Not determined.

CHROMIUM

Sources: Whole grain cereals, clams, corn oil, brewer's yeast.

Dietary role: Increases effectiveness of insulin; stimulates enzymes in metabolism of energy; healthy blood circulatory system; synthesis of fatty acids, cholesterol, and protein

Deficiency: Depressed growth rate, arteriosclerosis, and intolerance in diabetics.

COBALT

Sources: Leafy green vegetables, fruit, poultry, milk, clams, and organ meats.

Dietary role: Maintains red blood cells, functions as part of vitamin B12, and activates some enzymes in body.

Deficiency: Retarded growth rate and pernicious anemia.

COPPER

Sources: Soybeans, raisins, nuts, bonemeal, organ meats, fish, legumes, and molasses.

Dietary role: Part of many enzymes; works with vitamin C to form elastin; formation of red blood cells; color of hair and skin; good for bone formation.

Deficiency: Skin sores, impaired respiration, and general weakness.

IODINE

Sources: Mushrooms, iodized salt, fish, and seaweed.

Dietary role: Regulates energy production and rate of metabolism; enhances thyroid function and needed for prevention of goiter (a swelling of the thyroid gland). Also required for healthy hair, skin, nails, and teeth.

Deficiency: Obesity, irritability, dry hair, nervousness, cold hands and feet.

IRON

Sources: Cherry juice, liver, eggs, fish, wheatgerm, leafy green vegetables, fortified cereals, dried fruits, and poultry.

Dietary role: Formation of hemoglobin and myoglobin; promotes protein metabolism; stress and disease resistance; promotes growth; good for healthy teeth, skin, nails, bones

Deficiency: Weakness, difficulty in breathing, anemia, constipation, and brittle nails.

LITHIUM

Sources: Foods grown in mineral-rich soil.

Dietary role: Proper endocrine regulation; brain function; promoter of actin – a protein that stimulates the formation of muscle tissue.

Deficiency: Depressed growth, reduced fertility, reduced longevity, and depression.

MAGNESIUM

Sources: Molasses, whole grains, honey, nuts, seaweed, tuna, bran, green vegetables, bone meal, and fish.

Dietary role: Catalyst in the utilization of carbohydrates, fats, protein, phosphorus, calcium, and possibly potassium. Good for energy; healthy maintenance of bones, arteries, heart, nerves, and teeth.

Deficiency: Muscular excitability, confusion, nervousness, and tremors.

MANGANESE

Sources: Whole grains, nuts, legumes, leafy green vegetables, bananas, celery, pineapple, liver, and egg yolk.

Dietary role: Enzyme activation maintains sex hormone production; helps carbohydrate and fat production, tissue respiration; utilizes vitamin E; needed for normal skeletal development.

Deficiency: Hearing loss, ataxia, and dizziness.

MOLYBDENUM

Sources: Milk, dairy products, legumes, organ meats, and whole grains.

Dietary role: Proper mental function and amino acid metabolism.

Deficiency: Depressed growth, low appetite, impaired reproduction and fertility.

NICKEL

Sources: Dark chocolate (minimum 70 percent cocoa solids), nuts, dried beans, and grains.

Dietary role: Optimal growth, healthy skin, bone structure; enhances alkaline phosphate.

Deficiency: Depressed growth and dermatitis.

PHOSPHORUS

Sources: Legumes, milk products, bone meal, nuts, yellow cheese, eggs, fish, whole grains, and poultry.

Dietary role: Works with calcium to form bones, teeth; cell growth and repair; utilizes carbohydrate, fat, and protein; heart muscle contraction and nerve activity.

Deficiency: Pyorrhea, weight loss, appetite loss, irregular breathing, fatigue, nervousness, and weight problems.

POTASSIUM

Sources: Meats, whole grains, legumes, dried fruits, figs, peaches, nuts, seafood, bananas, and apricots.

Dietary role: Controls activity of heart muscles, nervous system, kidneys; rapid growth; muscle contractions; nerve tranquilization.

Deficiency: Respiratory failure; cardiac arrest; poor reflexes; dry skin; nervousness; irregular heartbeat (slow); and insomnia.

SELENIUM

Sources: Broccoli, onions, tuna, herring, bran and wheatgerm, brewer's yeast, and whole grains.

Dietary role: Works with vitamin E, preserves tissue elasticity, and utilizes proteins.

Deficiency: Premature aging.

SILICON

Sources: Unrefined high-fiber grains, cereals, and root vegetables.

Dietary role: Essential for the repair, maintenance, and formation of healthy connective tissue.

Deficiency: Impaired formation of bone and cartilage (low collagen content).

VANADIUM

Sources: Shellfish, mushrooms, parsley, dill seed, black pepper.

Dietary role: Regulation of energy production; inhibition of cholesterol synthesis. Enhances bone and tooth formation.

Deficiency: Impaired prenatal survival, depressed growth, plasma cholesterol, lipids and phospholipids.

ZINC

Sources: Organ meats, brewer's yeast, fish, soybeans, liver, spinach, mushrooms, and sunflower seeds.

Dietary role: Aids digestion and metabolism of phosphorus and protein. A component of insulin and male reproductive fluid, it also aids the prostate, and the burn and wound healing process.

Deficiency: Sterility, delayed sexual maturity, loss of taste, poor appetite, fatigue, and retarded growth.

CAUTION

You should get dietary advice from your medical practitioner before taking supplements.

If you implement the guidelines I have just outlined, you will feel much better very quickly, both physically and mentally. You will be preparing your body for a faster recovery from your stress and anxiety symptoms.

Foundations for stress-free living

◉ Eat small, regular meals and always carry a supply of healthy snacks (berries, oatcakes, nuts and seeds, raw veggies, fruits, etc.) so that you can top up your energy levels throughout the day. Remember, the more stressed you are, the more energy you are burning, so don't forget to refuel!

- Avoid alcohol and sugar-laden sodas and cordials: they spike your blood sugar levels and have little value in a healthy diet. Juices and smoothies are healthier, but stick to a glass or two a day and drink with food because they are high in natural sugars.

- Avoid eating heavy meals late at night. Instead, eat a small snack before going to bed to sustain you through the night.

- Aim for a diet that is low in refined sugars and saturated fats, high in slow-release carbohydrates, fruit and vegetables, good fats, and high-quality proteins found in dairy, fish, pulses, and legumes. Watch out for spicy foods, which can cause the digestive tract to struggle to maintain chemical equilibrium as they pass through the various digestive processes. Also avoid the hidden sugars in processed foods and low-fat diet foods (the fat has usually been replaced with sugar).

- Eat three large bananas a day, one about 30 minutes after each meal. You will be surprised how much more energy you will have.

 Day 2

HYDRATE, DON'T STIMULATE

As we discussed on Day 1, balancing your blood sugar is vital in helping you combat stress. But while many people are concerned about what they eat, it's also important to understand that what we drink (or don't) affects our physical and mental health, too.

Most of the time the odd cup of coffee, black tea, energy drink or cola won't have long-term negative effects, but during times of stress and worry, caffeine is one of the worst culprits for fuelling stress. Caffeine is a stimulant that affects the nervous system and makes you feel more alert; however, it also heightens anxiety levels and that's bad news for your stress levels.

If you drink more than 250 mg of caffeine a day (that's two cups of instant or one cup of filtered coffee, or two to four cups of tea – depending on the brew strength – or one can of cola or energy drink), you increase your risk of suffering from a range of unpleasant side effects, including:

- Nervousness
- Irritability
- Restlessness
- Insomnia
- Headaches
- Heart palpitations

If you regularly drink more than two cups of coffee, cola, or energy drinks, then it is likely that you're addicted to caffeine and simply removing this toxin from your diet will immediately reduce your stress levels and heighten your sense of wellbeing.

The best drink in the world – water

We've already discussed how overdosing on sugar-laden cordials and fruit smoothies is not a good idea, so what should you drink? Honestly, the best thing you can drink is diluted fruit juices or plain water. It might seem a little boring compared to a cappuccino or a cup of black tea, but water is vital for good health. It serves to carry substances (oxygen, hormones, vitamins, and minerals) around the body in the bloodstream. Water also acts as a lubricant in joints and helps control body temperature. It helps cleanse the body of waste products and poisons. In addition, we lose a lot of water in sweat, urine, and feces, and this must be replaced by drinking.

 Remember: stay hydrated
Dehydration – however slight – can cause anxious feelings, so make sure you drink plenty of fluids throughout the day.

Foundations for stress-free living

◉ Drink plenty of water (aim for five to seven glasses a day). You can flavor it with a dash of fresh lemon, orange, or lime juice, if you like.

◉ Food also contains water so make sure your diet contains plenty of fresh fruit and vegetables.

◉ Caffeinated drinks such as black tea, coffee, energy drinks, sugar-laden and sugar-free colas can make you jittery and anxious, so just avoid them. Replace them with water, diluted fruit juices, and herbal teas – especially chamomile, which is a very mild sedative.

◉ If you regularly consume caffeinated drinks you might find you develop some withdrawal symptoms over the next few days. Keep drinking plenty of water and these will pass quickly.

 # Day 3

ALCOHOL

Let me talk a little about alcohol and its effects. You may drink socially, regularly, or not at all, but even a small amount of alcohol can profoundly affect your stress and anxiety levels and is best avoided over the next 30 days. Just use common sense to apply this principal to your life… it will pay dividends.

The first question to ask about alcohol is, what is it and why does it make us feel THAT way?

The five stages of intoxication

Alcohol acts like an anesthetic: the more we drink the more of our brain is anesthetized. The most common explanation of how the intoxication process works is that the physiological abilities we learned last (e.g. social etiquette) are the first to be affected and those that we learned first (e.g. breathing) are the last to go. In essence, alcohol does these things to us because it's poisoning us… drink enough of it and the ultimate affect of the poison is experienced.

Stage one: Social lubricant

After a couple of drinks you'll probably experience an improved mood and perhaps feel merry. Your body reacts by increasing your heart rate, which in turn produces a mental 'high.' The effect of a raised blood-alcohol level causes the small capillaries in your skin to expand, which makes you blush and feel warmer, but also lowers your blood pressure.

Stage two: Spin

After a few more drinks, you'll probably start to feel lightheaded. Your physical function and reaction are heavily impaired and your ability to reason is affected. These effects are caused by the action of the alcohol on the nervous system.

Stage three: Intoxication

This stage is reached after a few more drinks. Reaction times reduce, speech is slurred, and vision severely impaired. The liver becomes seriously overloaded and struggles to rid the blood of the dangerous levels of alcohol that have been consumed. With correct care, your liver should repair itself, but it will struggle to do so effectively after many repetitions of this damage.

Stage four: Cab?

Now you can hardly walk; you bump into everyone and everything in your path. No one can understand you… or wants to!

Your body is rejecting the poisonous alcohol, and you constantly need to urinate as it subconsciously decides to release the poison in self-preservation. Your body is dehydrating, exacerbating the effect of the alcohol; this is what causes the inevitable 'hangover' and headaches.

Your stomach and intestines struggle to handle the dehydration, too – you get stomach cramps, diarrhea, and sickness as your body tries to reject the poison.

Stage five: On the edge of existence

This stage requires no explanation. The body struggles to stay conscious and is one step away from failing completely! No man's land!

So, what is alcohol?

Alcohol is a lethal poison that can kill in just a few hours. Sure, it can make you feel good temporarily, but in the long term the effects can be shocking and no one knows what their level of tolerance is: stage five intoxication for one grown man might be six glasses of wine, while for another it might be a single chocolate liqueur. Add to this very unappealing picture the fact that many people are alcohol sensitive and even allergic, and the whole thing starts to look very unpleasant indeed.

One of the main issues facing regular drinkers is that the body can respond differently each time they drink, and there are many examples of seasoned drinkers coming to harm having drunk relatively small quantities. It is this unpredictability that causes the majority of catastrophic outcomes.

Whether you drink every day or in larger quantities over short periods, alcohol can cause anxiety and stress levels to fluctuate dramatically. Many people find that wine is often the worst culprit, and during times of high anxiety and stress, it causes much more pronounced symptoms, but any alcohol can cause similar effects.

Alcohol contains high levels of sugar, which has obvious negative effects on our health and blood sugar levels, as discussed in the previous chapter. The psychological effects of the experience of being drunk or tipsy can also alter our perception of the world in a way that can cause higher levels of sadness, worry, and other emotions. Alcohol consumption should always be minimized for maintaining general good health, but in anxiety conditions and times of stress, it is advisable to abstain completely.

If you drink alcohol regularly, this far outweighs the health benefits that drinking small quantities may bring. The rates of serious illness are massively higher among regular drinkers, while the health benefits of drinking two or three units of red wine each week are very widely documented.

So what is a healthy balance? Well, as I have said, two to three small glasses of wine per week. What about beer and spirits? Well, my advice is to avoid them completely. Beer is full of sugar, and spirits are usually mixed with a sugary drink, so they have little or no beneficial effect on your health. Alcohol has such a profound effect on us because it adversely affects us, not because it creates positive changes.

🦋 Remember: alcohol creates anxiety and stress
ALCOHOL is NOT helping to 'drown your sorrows'… it can't. It actually has depressant qualities, which not only make your mood even worse, but ultimately make you wake up the next day feeling worse, too.

Foundations for stress-free living

◉ Minimize your alcohol intake and drink more water-based drinks without extra sugar instead. You will notice the benefits very quickly indeed.

◉ Maintain a healthy diet that is high in mood-enhancing foods, such as leafy green vegetables, high-quality proteins, and good fats (e.g. olive oil, avocados, and nuts).

◉ If you stop drinking for one month from today, you'll feel fitter, healthier, less tired, and more able to cope with everything life throws at you. Try it, you won't be disappointed. That I assure you!

◉ If you usually have, for example, ten drinks on a Friday night, reduce that by half. If you have two or more drinks every day, reduce the quantity by half. When this new routine feels comfortable, reduce your intake to a quarter of what you used to drink, and so on.

◉ Change your routine to avoid those times when you drink. So, if you always have a couple of drinks before dinner, use that time to take a relaxing bath or an invigorating shower, to lie down and relax, or take some gentle exercise.

◉ Keep the money you save by not drinking and use it to treat yourself to a massage, the latest must-have gadget, or anything that makes you feel good.

◉ Remember: alcohol is the number one cause of unhappiness in our society.

 # Day 4

ANXIETY... WHAT IS IT?

Before I tell you about anxiety and the symptoms and thoughts it can cause, let me first tell you that most doctors describe anxiety-type symptoms as stress or even depression.

This isn't laziness, or the fact that doctors are misinformed about the medical realities of the condition, it is simply that, from a doctor's perspective, stress and anxiety seem to go hand in hand. Many people suffering from high anxiety have come to me with a diagnosis of stress or depression from their medical practitioner. The whole field is just a bit fuzzy, but I will explain why the three conditions are so, so different.

Stress, depression, and anxiety

Stress is a condition resulting from the pressures of life and work. To say it's an illness would be wrong. It's not. Stress is a group of symptoms that affect sufferers both physically and mentally, and render them unable to cope as efficiently as they did before. Why? Because when work and life pressure conspire to form the condition of stress, it also becomes a high-anxiety condition.

The symptoms of stress are wide ranging, because they are also the symptoms of anxiety. But, if they are addressed early enough, all stress symptoms can be eliminated.

Before I tell you what anxiety is, let me tell you what it is not. It is most definitely not depression. Depression is a condition thought to be due to a chemical imbalance in the brain that robs the sufferer of the experiences of emotion. In essence, they feel numb to all emotion. Depression sufferers don't experience any emotional outpouring that would make them care about, well, pretty much anything. However, depression can be treated effectively with guided life-coaching practices, and it is believed that antidepressants offer a curative solution; for me, however, the jury is still out on that one.

Anxiety, in complete polar opposition to depression, is total sensory hyper-vigilance, by which I mean if depression is a complete suppression of emotion, anxiety is the complete opposite. Anxiety sufferers, unlike depressed people, experience an often constant group of physical and mental 'symptoms' that prepare the body for 'fight or flight' (see page xviii) and also create a massively embellished experience of the world through over-sensitized senses – all caused by the activation of the emotion of fear.

What is anxiety, then? Well, it's any experience of sensations and thoughts that are present when we perceive threat, but for many people it's more than that.

We have all experienced anxiety at one time or another and when it is appropriate, it forms part of the most important human defense systems. When anxiety is required it can produce miraculous physical and mental strength, but when inappropriate it can cause phobias, panic disorder, multiple symptoms, post-traumatic stress disorder, and obsessive-compulsive disorder.

The symptoms associated with anxiety disorders can range from mild shyness to extreme panic disorder. They can be varied – from dizziness or breathlessness to muscle tremors, and from digestive problems to headaches – and the list is almost endless. However, anxiety disorders feature physical anxiety symptoms such as:

- Smothering sensations and shortness of breath
- Racing heart, slow heart beat, palpitations
- Chest pains
- 'Lump in throat' and difficulty swallowing (*globus hystericus*)
- Blanching (color loss in the skin)
- Excessive perspiration (sweating)
- Shaking or shivering (visibly or internally)
- Pain or numbness in the head, face, neck, or shoulders
- Rapid gastric emptying
- Indigestion, heartburn, constipation, and diarrhea
- Sexual dysfunction
- Symptoms of urinary tract infection
- Skin rashes
- Weakness/tingling in arms, hands, or feet

- 'Electric shock' feelings (anywhere in the body)

- Dry mouth

- Flu-like symptoms

- Distorted vision

- Disturbed hearing

- Hormone problems

- Headaches and feelings of having a 'tight band around head'

- Sore eyes

- 'Creeping' or 'pins and needles' sensations in the skin

- Increased sensitivity to light, sound, touch, and smell

- Pain in the face or jaw (resembling toothache)

There are also psychological anxiety symptoms such as:

- Insomnia

- Nightmares

- Fears of going mad or losing control

- Increased depression and suicidal feelings

- Aggression

- Agoraphobia

- Hallucinations

- Hyperactivity

- Dramatic increase in sexual feelings

- Obsessive thoughts, often aggressive, sexual, or religious in nature

- Derealization and depersonalization

How does an anxiety disorder form?

First of all, let me tell you that anxiety disorders are not mental or physical illnesses, they are behavioral conditions, which means that they have developed as a result of a modification of YOUR thoughts and/or actions; they cannot form in any other way!

The catalyst for an anxiety disorder is produced when an initial anxious reaction causes changes to take place deep inside the brain. This 'learning process' etches behavioral changes into your subconscious mind called 'neuroplasticity.' In other words, the more anxious the person becomes, the more the body and mind take on that new level of anxiety as the 'normal' level. In the same way that practicing driving eventually leads to being able to do it relatively naturally and with very little conscious attention to the action required to maneuver the car and navigate the road ahead.

You will recognize an anxiety disorder as being different from stress because stress comes and goes as life circumstances change. During those times you may display anxious behaviors, but an anxiety disorder puts you in a constant state of heightened stress.

Anxiety disorders form when the emotion of fear is constant. Anxiety disorders, including generalized anxiety disorder, panic disorder, agoraphobia, OCD, pure O, post-traumatic stress disorder, depersonalization and derealization, form when the emotion of fear isn't deactivated.

Anxiety disorders are caused by the combination of two factors: the sufferer having creative intellect, an advanced level of creative ability above the human 'norm,' and an initiating anxiety catalyst, which can be any life event that raised the anxiety level. Once the anxiety response is activated and an inappropriate response to it is created, due to the person's creatively embellished response, the resultant anxiety disorder can last for decades as the sufferer becomes a slave to the behaviors that minimize their activities and protect the anxiety.

I believe that anxiety disorders are at pandemic proportions and are the most catastrophic health-related conditions in the world. Their social and economic wake affects more people than any other health-related issue. This is why The Linden Method is so unique: it quickly reverses the subconscious changes made by anxiety and permanently eliminates the anxiety disorder at its source.

CASE HISTORY *Louise, aged 20, student*

Louise suffered from shyness and mild anxiety throughout her childhood, but at university she started to experience heightened anxiety, accompanied by inappropriate thoughts about the people around her. She would imagine aggressive or sexual encounters with her close family, for example, and over time she became more and more reclusive. Louise had many friends and an active social life, but within three months, she was rarely leaving the house, and became agoraphobic (experiencing extreme anxiety and, occasionally, panic attacks when she tried to leave home or travel anywhere alone). What many sufferers don't know is that these inappropriate anxious thoughts are part of the anxiety response, risk assessments done as the brain uses the body's senses to detect and deal with threats. Louise had no idea what the thoughts were, and so she feared them and her anxiety was constantly exacerbated. Louise's family became concerned about her and contacted us. Louise attended one of our workshops, used the Anxiety Recovery Program and within days, was feeling reassured and substantially less anxious. Within a month, Louise was back at university and her high-anxiety condition had gone. She graduated last year and is currently volunteering in Africa.

Predisposed to stress

My unique view is that there is a group of people who are born with a predisposition to developing a high-anxiety condition. That's not to say they are predestined to develop an anxiety condition, simply that, when their life circumstances conspire to produce an anxious catalyst, THEY above people without the predisposition, can develop an anxiety disorder. There are those who could never develop an anxiety condition. So what is this trait?

As I mentioned previously, there has been a genetic and sociological 'train crash' during human evolution. There have been a number of these, but this one seems to be the most catastrophic and far-reaching, causing the previously mentioned anxiety pandemic. Billions of people suffer from high-anxiety conditions and they can be cured simply and effectively.

I call the genetic trait 'creative intellect,' and the train crash is the interaction of an anxiety sufferer's creative intellect and their anxiety mechanism in the subconscious part of their mind.

You see, the anxiety response relies on the creativity center in the brain. The anxiety response produces risk assessments that 'look at' your environment, both external and inside your body, and then use creativity to discover the 'worst case scenario.' This means that everything your senses perceive is fed back to your subconscious mind and it does a calculation that goes something like this:

1   What have I found?

2   What does that mean to me?

3   What risk does it pose?

4   What is the worst outcome in this situation?

5   What is the most appropriate response to prevent risk to me?

Once the mind has answered these questions, it activates the body to take action. ALL of this happens subconsciously and entirely outside of your conscious control. The problem is that people with creative intellect don't stop there; their subconscious continues asking questions and making decisions in their defense:

1   I know the original threat has gone, but what else can I find?

2   What is this racing heart, palpitations, dizziness, muscle tightness, blurred vision [*or any other anxiety-related symptoms*]?

3   It could be a… heart attack, stroke, tumor, cancer [*or any other catastrophic health conditions*].

4   This could be a risk.

5   How do I respond to risk? ANXIETY RESPONSE.

Once the risk is detected (subconsciously), the anxiety response is reactivated and an anxiety disorder develops. Risk assessments finding symptoms and causing anxiety, anxiety causing symptoms and so on.

It may be that this affects you mostly when you have to make speeches or go on stage, but you may also have noticed that your general anxiety level is intrusive, making you feel anxious when you shouldn't. Regardless of what level of anxiety you experience, if the anxiety isn't appropriate to the situation you are in, you have an anxiety disorder.

Obsessive thoughts, leading to OCD and pure O, are a symptom of anxiety disorder, as are panic attacks and phobias. However, if you remove the underlying inappropriate anxiety, panic attacks, phobias, and obsessions cannot exist. FACT!

If you think that your anxiety will just go away, you may be correct, because in some cases it does, if life circumstances conspire to bring about recovery. However, there are quite a number of influential factors that need to be addressed simultaneously in order to make a full and permanent recovery, without which the chances of full recovery are very slim indeed. You don't have to rely on chance!

 Remember: anxiety recovery is a natural process
Structure, reassurance, knowledge, and support are the four key words when addressing anxiety issues, and our experience has shown that by combining these four elements correctly, a full recovery is inevitable.

◉ **Structure:** *Creating a specific daily schedule that supports anxiety recovery by reducing anxiety levels back down to your pre-set level at birth.*

◉ **Reassurance:** *This can only be provided by people who have the ability to correctly communicate proven information based on both their firsthand experiences with anxiety and with the knowledge gathered from helping many people. In addition, their knowledge and training must provide the correct answers to client's questions without pausing, in order to build trust and reassurance.*

◉ **Knowledge:** *Understand what anxiety is, and that it's a physical reaction, not a mental illness. Understand also that anxiety produces sensations and thoughts, not symptoms of an illness. Understand the physiology of the anxiety response and why the sensations and thoughts are appropriate, albeit unpleasant.*

◉ **Support:** *In order to recover quickly and permanently, it is vital that, when necessary, the sufferer receives the correct guidance and coaching in order to remain compliant.*

It is key that these four elements are present in order for the process to be simple, fast, and permanent. Children as young as seven have done The Linden Method with ease, and experienced fast and permanent results.

Like all learning processes, be it learning to play an instrument, to drive, to read or to write, it is vital that the process is carried out with compliance and with consistency in order for the process to be stored correctly in the brain. Anxiety recovery is no exception, except that anxiety recovery is far simpler than learning to read or write because it is a natural process that your brain does naturally; all we do is show people how to force it to happen.

Managing anxiety

If you think you need more help in managing your anxiety, then The Linden Method can help you (see the 'Resources' panel on pages 43–44), but in the meantime, I have brought together some tips to help you understand and manage your anxiety levels. These aren't a curative pathway, because this must be multifaceted and supported; however, these tips will help you to manage your anxiety effectively.

Exercise

Don't do things that push your heart rate too high. While this is harmless, and exercise is usually a great way to improve your fitness levels, during high anxiety, your mind doesn't understand the difference between exercise-induced changes to heart rate and those activated by your anxiety. When the mind receives signals that the heart is racing, it tends to see this as a risk and activates your anxiety response. Keep exercise at a lower level – walking rather than running and using lighter weights with more repetitions.

Stimulants

Coffee, tea, nicotine, and energy (including protein) drinks are all stimulants, and everyone understands the issues that can arise from taking illicit substances such as ecstasy, marijuana, and the many 'recreational' pills now available. Need I explain the issues that can arise when a person takes these substances? You are altering your body and mind chemistry when you take these substances, and while some stimulate your system, all, without exception, can increase your anxiety levels. If you take these substances, reduce slowly and then stop. It is vital that you create physical and psychological equilibrium in every one of your bodily systems, as without this foundation on which to build, recovery won't come easily.

Breathing

Despite what you may have been led to believe, you cannot cure an anxiety disorder by correcting your breathing. High anxiety levels affect breathing, but incorrect breathing isn't the cause of high anxiety! Meditation, relaxation exercises, and visualization are all great ways to relax and slow your breathing, but many sufferers find their anxiety cuts through any hope of relaxing, and that focusing on their breathing and their bodies can often make their anxiety much worse. Your breathing will return to normal as your anxiety disorder retreats but, in the meantime, the shortness of breath, smothering sensations and irregular breathing are a feature of high anxiety; it feels strange, but it's completely normal and harmless.

Blood sugar levels and diet

In order to create the physical and psychological equilibrium you will require as a foundation for recovery, it is vital that you maintain a constant, healthy blood sugar level. The endocrine system that controls hormones is heavily implicated in the management of your blood sugar levels as it controls insulin levels. However, the endocrine system also maintains a balance of interacting chemical messengers, and allowing blood sugar levels to fluctuate can produce quite significant changes in the way you feel and also the activation of the hormone adrenalin, which gives rise to anxiety. Eat little and often, don't eat too many carbohydrates, eat more protein, and follow the guidelines given on Day 1 (pages 1–19).

Managing your psychology

Physiology and psychology work in synchronized harmony, but when stress and anxiety causes disharmony, it can be very difficult indeed to accept the thoughts that accompany the physical symptoms. Thoughts come stronger and faster during high anxiety, but utilizing your intellect in a way that focuses the thoughts away from your physical self can slow them. During periods of high anxiety, it is useful to do things that utilize your intellect effectively, so find challenging tasks and try to create daily schedules that prevent you from becoming bored or unfocused.

Resources

The Linden Method eliminates anxiety disorders by using a group of simple but effective techniques in a structured program that takes no time or effort to implement – recovery just happens. If you are human and have high anxiety, it really can't fail. The Linden Method is the solution to any inappropriate anxiety – panic attacks, phobias, agoraphobia, PTSD, pure O, and OCD. Even sufferers of depression benefit hugely, reporting in many cases total elimination of their depressive thoughts and symptoms.

We currently have centers in the USA, UK, Germany, Spain, and Denmark. We also run residential retreats and workshops and have apps on iTunes. The team of qualified psychologists, psychotherapists, and anxiety recovery specialists is available to guide, reassure, and educate sufferers, and the curative success is second to none. To learn more about or to join our program, visit one of our websites (see page 199).

Foundations for stress-free living

- Each day, take 10–20 minutes to tune out the world and use the 'Deep Relaxation' visualization on the accompanying CD. Find somewhere quiet, comfortable, and warm to lie down and just allow time to relax. Calming your body also calms your mind and this simple exercise done daily will begin to retrain your mind and body to find a place of stillness and peace.

- Focus on eating healthily and avoiding stimulants, e.g. sugar, nicotine, caffeine, energy drinks, recreational drugs, and alcohol.

- Get plenty of rest and sleep. See also Day 9 (pages 69–74).

- Create some time for gentle exercise, e.g. tai chi or yoga. See also Day 7 (pages 55–59).

- Structure, reassurance, knowledge, and support are the key words when addressing anxiety issues, and our experience of those people using The Linden Method has shown that by combining these four elements correctly, a full recovery is inevitable.

 # Day 5

SMOKING! DO YOU OR DON'T YOU?

You may not smoke... if you don't, this section isn't for you... but, if you do, this IS for you, and it's important!

Smoking can cause blood sugar fluctuations, and also bodily changes caused by its stimulant properties. Smoking cessation is also not advisable during times of high anxiety; adding nicotine withdrawal to the anxiety you are experiencing could be very counter-productive indeed. If you smoke regularly, minimize the daily amount. If you smoke occasionally, stop completely if you feel you can do so with ease.

Resources: Getting help to quit

Many healthcare providers recommend nicotine replacement treatment (NRT) or smoking-cessation drugs (e.g. Champix) to help people quit smoking. However, the fundamental problem with these pharmaceutical methods is that they mask nicotine withdrawal symptoms but don't tackle the underlying problem: psychological dependence on cigarettes and nicotine. More effective, drug-free alternatives use cognitive and hypnotherapy approaches, and one approach that we've found works well is Allen Carr's method (for more information visit www.karmamind.com). Allen Carr's program aims to create 'happy non-smokers,' and focuses on shifting how smokers think and feel about smoking – no scare tactics, weight gain, or deprivation involved. You can even smoke during the program, and it has worked for more than five million people worldwide.

Many smokers will say that a cigarette calms them down, but this is physically impossible because nicotine is a stimulant and by feeding your body nicotine you are actually raising your stress levels. Smoking (and nicotine products) does affect your anxiety levels, and therefore your stress levels too. By eliminating the negative effects of nicotine, you will be adding to the balance you need in order to provide a solid foundation on which to eliminate stress completely.

Habits are the negative manifestation of instinctual behavior that you carry out without much or any conscious thought, and smoking is no exception. By eliminating negative habits from your life, you gain greater control over your subconscious. It's almost like cleaning out your attic: the emptier it is, the less it weighs down on your house.

Because smoking affects the way you breathe, it can negatively affect the rate and depth of breath, which is pre-set in every person. Stress and anxiety can be brought on by breathing, and controlled effectively using breathing exercises; it stands to reason that smoking can affect anxiety for this reason.

So, what's the plan? If you currently smoke more than ten cigarettes a day, try to cut down to ten. Once you have done this, it is vital that you then allow your body to become balanced. Your body will be acclimatized to the nicotine it currently receives, so it may be uncomfortable for a few days, but, ultimately, it will pay dividends. If you smoke less that ten cigarettes a day, estimate how many and stick to that quantity. Again, the key here is balance! Remember that any fluctuations in body chemicals, including nicotine or alcohol (in fact anything we ingest), can cause profound sensations and withdrawal.

You can address your smoking habit later when you feel stronger, but for the time being, create balance and control in order to allow your body to recover.

Replace negative habits with positive ones; become passionate about something that will enrich your life, challenge you, and ultimately create a feeling of fulfillment.

 Remember: five minutes is all it takes...

The next time you find yourself craving a nicotine fix, check your watch and allow yourself just five minutes to dwell on those negative thoughts. Once those five minutes are up, you would have finished smoking the cigarette that you were craving. The process is over, so forget about it and move on!

Foundations for stress-free living

⊙ Although many people believe that a cigarette calms them down, nicotine is a stimulant and creates additional stress and anxiety within the body. Instead, keep using the 'Deep Relaxation' visualization on the CD, as you may find it helpful for cutting down on those pesky cigarettes.

- You don't need to be told that cigarette smoking is bad for your health, but when you're undergoing extreme stress or, particularly, anxiety, don't add to your woes by quitting smoking. Set a quit date and aim to stop smoking when you've overcome your anxiety and stress issues.

- Nicotine depletes levels of vitamins B, C, and D, so take a high-dose daily multi-vitamin supplement. This works in two ways: it will help restore the negative effects of nicotine within your body and help to reduce cravings.

- Reducing your nicotine intake can leave you feeling tired and irritable, but supplementing with caffeine and sugar (both stimulants) is not the answer and will exacerbate any existing stress or anxiety. Instead, make sure you get plenty of sleep, drink seven to eight glasses of clear fluids (water and diluted fruit juices) every day, and eat a high-quality diet rich in B, C, and D vitamins (citrus fruits, leafy green vegetables, nuts and seeds, eggs, and oily fish).

- Cigarette smoking is a behavior as well as an addiction, and so varying your routine can help you avoid those times when you smoke out of habit rather than need. For example, if you always have a cup of coffee and a cigarette as soon as you wake up, switch to a glass of fresh orange juice and do some stretching exercises first. Or, if you always have a cigarette after eating, take a brisk walk or do the dishes before having your smoke. The key is to vary your routine and show your brain that you can do things differently. Start creating new habits.

- Don't beat yourself up about smoking, but do start thinking how great it will feel when you put out that final cigarette and free yourself from nicotine addiction. Thousands of people quit smoking successfully every year, and you can do it too.

 # Day 6

BREATHING

Do you breathe correctly?

I bet you don't. Most people just breathe; it doesn't need to be a conscious thing, it just happens... right? To an extent that's true – the autonomic nervous system takes over breathing for us and generally it serves its purpose. Sometimes, however, breathing can become disrupted by stress, anxiety, exercise, posture, or digestive issues, and it is then that we notice the adverse effects that breathing has on the way we feel.

Breathing can even affect the way we think. The brain can become disoriented and confused by minute changes in oxygen supply, which can lead to drowsiness, confusion, and other non-specific symptoms – harmless, but embarrassing and frustrating for some people.

So, I ask you again, do you think you breathe correctly?

Daily breathing exercises

There are a number of very good resources and practices that are helpful in teaching you to breathe efficiently – e.g. tai chi, yoga, and Pilates – but using a simple breathing exercise daily can be very beneficial indeed.

Breathing exercise: 3:2 technique

The 3:2 technique is a very simple exercise and should form the foundation of your normal breathing technique. Of course, if you're carrying a little extra weight or are unfit, this may take some practice, but it should become easier in time.

Put on some loose-fitting clothing and then sit comfortably in a straight-backed chair in a warm place where you won't be disturbed.

The perfect ratio of in to out breathing is 3:2, so count three in and two out over a 60-second period. Before you start, make sure that you understand how a breath should feel. Place one hand in the center of your chest and the other on your belly (below your naval). Now breathe in. You should feel expansion in both your belly and your chest equally. This means that your lungs are inflating effectively and optimizing the efficiency of oxygen intake.

To start with, you should be practicing this twice a day before eating, and for approximately ten minutes each session until it feels natural, and then increase by five minutes every week until you are able to breathe in this way for an hour or more. At this point you'll be feeling very comfortable with this routine. Now you can start to implement this breathing routine as your 'normal' breathing pattern.

While doing this exercise, you could listen to relaxing music and close your eyes if you wish; the meditative element of doing this can be very relaxing indeed, and the time will pass quicker. Try to make time to do this exercise every day. Just a minute or two of correct breathing can energize you and relax you in times of stress.

The beauty of the 3:2 exercise is that it can be done as easily in bed as when you're at work or waiting for a bus, and the benefits of mastering it can be massive. By being in control of your breath, you feed your brain oxygen, promote internal calmness, control the fight-or-flight or anxiety response, and prevent stress-related conditions from developing, so the physical and mental health benefits are enormous.

 ### Remember: managing stress
Understand that breathing exercises or adjustments do not cure stress or high anxiety, but may help you to minimize their impact while you work on adjusting other aspects of your life practice as outlined in this book.

Breathing exercise: Sleep squeeze

Another breathing exercise that is excellent if you're having trouble falling asleep is what I call the 'sleep squeeze,' and it's very simple to do.

Lie down on your bed, on your back is best. Now take a deep, slow breath in through your nose, and at the same time, squeeze your toes tightly as if you are trying to curl them under your foot, then release the squeeze.

Then do the same again, this time curling your foot up toward your knee. Then do the same again, contracting your calf muscles, then your thighs, buttocks, belly, chest, arms, and so on until you have moved all the way up your body, squeezing and releasing the muscles one by one.

When you have tensed and released every muscle you can, from head to toe, your breathing should be much more steady and you should feel ready for sleep. If not, repeat the exercise.

Breathing exercise: Deep breaths

Lie down on your bed. Take a deep, slow breath in to the count of three and then exhale. On exhaling, imagine that you are sinking into your bed, as if gravity itself is pulling you deeper into the mattress.

Repeat this exercise 20 times, using slow, rhythmic breaths, and each time imagining that you're sinking deeper and deeper into the mattress.

As with the sleep squeeze, this exercise is also useful if you are feeling stressed or finding it difficult to fall asleep.

Resources

We'll be talking more about exercise on Day 7 (see pages 55–59), but I would also highly recommend learning an exercise that promotes energizing breath and movement, such as tai chi or yoga, both of which use breathing techniques, meditation, and controlled movement to promote stress reduction and anxiety elimination. Both can be practiced just once or twice a week, and the benefits are great. If you can't find a suitable class there are lots of great DVDs and web-based tutorials available.

Foundations for stress-free living

- A diet high in dairy products can create extra (and unwanted) mucus, which can affect your breath and lungs. This is because dairy products contain casein – a sticky substance that can leave you feeling plugged up. If this sounds familiar, then it might be worth asking your doctor to test you for sensitivity to dairy products. Alternatively, cut down your dairy intake for a week and see how your body responds.

- Smoking obviously affects your ability to breathe, but using the techniques outlined above can also help you reduce how much you smoke. As you breathe deeply, you begin to realize how 'good' it feels just to breathe oxygen, and in turn how it brings you a sense of calm and ease that could never be achieved by smoking a cigarette. See also, Day 5 (pages 45–48).

- If you're carrying extra weight this will affect your ability to breathe, and so it is even more important to practice the 3:2 technique. You may also find that bringing some times of 'controlled breathing' and relaxation into your life will help you lose weight as part of a sensible healthy eating plan. Many people suffer from 'emotional eating' in response to stress. Using the methods outlined in this book will help you overcome this issue.

- When you take control of your breath it sends a signal to your brain that all is well in the world, which in turn has a positive effect on your ability to deal with stressful situations, so use the breath exercises daily.

Day 7

EXERCISE

You probably already know that exercise is an important element of maintaining good health, but what you might consider strenuous could be a walk in the park for die-hard exercisers.

If you are experiencing high levels of anxiety or stress, it is advisable to choose exercises that don't raise the heart rate more than 20–30 beats per minute above your resting heart rate. Doing exercise doesn't mean that you have to send your heart racing like a steam train; exercise should just raise your heart rate to a comfortable level. You don't need to overdo it to experience the benefits.

In many cases, anxiety levels and stress can be adversely affected by strenuous exercise. Walking, cycling, and swimming are the best forms of exercise during high anxiety, but you must monitor how they make you feel (and this will be dependent on your fitness levels.)

Remember: recommended physical activity levels
Taking too much strenuous exercise can be as damaging to your stress levels as taking too little, because it stresses out your adrenals (your body's management system for coping with stress). It's a good idea to aim for the following levels of exercise, but to avoid exceeding them: young people (5–18 years) should exercise for about 60 minutes a day, while those aged 19 or older should exercise for 150 minutes a week.

What's the best exercise?

Treating tens of thousands of people with stress and anxiety over the last decade has revealed to us the sort of exercise regimes that are most beneficial to sufferers in order to reverse the effects of stress, strengthen the body, and improve cardiovascular function, but are also enjoyable and relaxing. There are two types of exercise program that fall into this group and are particularly useful – tai chi and yoga. Both are summarized below.

Tai chi

Tai chi is a low-impact exercise suitable for people of all levels of fitness. In fact, it has been shown to be particularly helpful for people suffering with joint issues (e.g. osteoporosis and arthritis) and the elderly. Studies indicate that tai chi is helpful in improving mobility and balance, increasing strength, and, most importantly, reducing stress. Slow and graceful movement characterizes tai chi, as the practitioner flows seamlessly between a series of poses known as a 'form' or 'pattern.' Most of the movements are carried out with slightly bent knees in a squat-like posture or stance. There are a number of variants or styles to choose from, but most of the differences between the styles involve variations in the hand positions, and all types of tai chi carry similar health benefits.

Yoga

While there is still more scope for scientific research, dozens of studies have shown the health benefits of yoga, and it is suitable for everyone, whatever their level of fitness. There are several forms of yoga (For example Hatha, Ashtanga, Sivananda) and it's important to choose a type that is suitable for your level of fitness. Many classes often finish with a breathing and relaxation exercise, but the main emphasis of yoga is a series of postures that focus on breath, strength, and balance.

Resources

Before signing up for a class, it's always better to try something at home. I recommend two DVDs: John Scott's Ashtanga Yoga *and Desiree Bartlett's* Yoga for Beginners *(both available at www.karmamind.com), which many of my clients use as an introduction. Many clients continue to use the DVDs at this level, while others decide to take their knowledge further by joining a class or taking private tuition. Most instructors will let you try a class for free to find out whether it's suitable for you.*

Both yoga and tai chi are incredibly effective at providing everything that every person of every age would want from an exercise program. Both are simple to do, don't require you to leave home, can be done alone or with a friend, can be intensified if required, and include breathing techniques and meditation/visualization. In addition, once you have become moderately good at them, you can use them for just five or ten minutes each day with dramatic effects. Although neither exercise will help you lose weight (if that's what you require) they are effective at reducing stress levels, which in turn can have a positive influence on your diet.

 Remember: simplicity is key

Many of my clients now do regular tai chi and yoga exercises. The beauty of these exercises is that you can step out of bed and do two or three before breakfast to prepare yourself for the day ahead, AND they can be done at work or at home when required!

Foundations for stress-free living

◉ The advantages of tai chi and yoga are numerous: balance, posture, breathing, joint strength and flexibility, and most importantly, reduced stress levels.

◉ Many people blame a lack of time for their inability to exercise, so take advantage of technology and exercise at home by using a DVD. If you have a partner and/or children, you could always make it a family event and get everyone involved in your new workout program.

◉ There are many simple ways to increase the amount of low-impact exercise in your life, and here are just a few suggestions. Get off the bus a stop or two earlier and lengthen your walk to work every day. If you have to do a school run every day, walk rather than take the car, or park and walk part of the way. If you're visiting a shopping mall or grocery store, park further away so you have to do some walking to get to the store. Take the kids to the park after school for a runaround. Spend 20 minutes of your lunch break walking around a local park or green space. Put on some gentle music and dance while getting on with the household chores (just ignore any rude remarks from your family).

⊙ Get an exercise buddy: a pact to exercise with a likeminded friend can really help you maintain a gentle exercise routine, as well as give you valuable 'YOU time.' See also Day 18 (see pages 121–126).

⊙ Taking regular, gentle exercise is vital for combating stress, and, combined with a healthy eating program and avoiding stimulants and alcohol, should give you positive results instantly. If you have already brought some of these ideas into play, you should be feeling calmer, more able to cope with stress, and ready to get your body moving.

 # Day 8

PANIC ATTACKS

When we experience excessive levels of stress, which will be different for everyone, the body responds with an ancient inbuilt response known as 'fight or flight,' and causes many physical symptoms including:

◉ Increased respiratory and cardiac rate.

◉ Constriction of blood vessels (in certain parts of the body) and dilation of blood vessels in the limbs and muscles.

◉ Digestion action slows or stops, as blood is diverted (along with nutrients) to the muscles and limbs.

◉ Pupil dilation and/or loss of peripheral vision.

◉ Loss of hearing.

◉ Inhibition of the lachrymal glands, which are responsible for tear production.

These are all very useful physical responses for situations of 'real' danger, but fairly useless when it comes to the day-to-day stresses of modern living. However, for some people, the fight-or-flight response can develop into panic attacks, which you may or may not have experienced. If you have, today's session is for you. If not, thank your lucky stars and look forward to tomorrow's session. Or read on, because you may find this valuable for someone you know who does suffer.

If you have recently – for example, within the last three months – experienced a panic attack, chances are that you have not yet tackled the subconscious anxious reaction that causes them. Do you ever feel anxious? Do you feel inappropriately anxious to the point of experiencing physical symptoms?

Panic attacks are the most extreme physical manifestation of anxiety or stress. They can build slowly or hit hard and unexpectedly. Usually, panic attacks cause a number of common symptoms, including:

- Chest pains
- Shortness of breath (hyperventilation)
- Sweating
- Shaking
- Faintness
- Racing heart
- Pins and needles in the extremities
- Feeling dreamy, detached, or unreal
- Agitation
- Weird thoughts (for example, paranoia, feelings of impending doom)

CASE HISTORY *Brian, aged 42, salesperson*

Brian worked for a national car leasing company and, following a long period of stress at work and home – and a particularly alcohol-fuelled night out – he found himself in the hospital ER with chest pains, shortness of breath, sweating, shaking, and dizziness. Fearing the worst, his friends had called an ambulance after they found him in the bar's bathroom, splashing his face with water and looking unwell and scared. As with the many thousands of people with stories like this that we hear about and treat, Brian had experienced a massive panic attack and went on to develop a severe panic disorder.

Two years later, Brian was taking a cocktail of anti-depressants and sedatives. His case was overseen by the local mental health team, who provided him with CBT (cognitive behavioral therapy) and taught him some relaxation techniques, but with no success at all. In fact, he was getting worse. Brian had lost his job and was a massive drain on his wife's health, played no active role in bringing up their four children, or helping around the house. He had become as dependent on his wife as his children were. In desperation, his wife searched online and found The Linden Method website. She immediately called the team and signed him up for our home learning program. Brian used the 'Panic Attack Eliminator' audio track contained in our program materials, and his panic attacks stopped immediately.

Over the following months Brian and his wife received support from our staff. By the third month Brian was back in a new job, assisting his wife, and being a great dad again. Brian's anxiety and panic attacks were completely gone within weeks, and he started withdrawing from the medications with assistance from our support team.

Are panic attacks harmful?

Panic attacks are not harmful; they just feel very frightening. Panic attacks occur when adrenalin is released by the adrenal glands as a reaction to the perception of extreme danger… when danger truly exists, adrenalin and the anxious reaction are valuable parts of our natural defense system, which prepares us for 'fight or flight.' However, if this reaction happens when NO danger is present, it is called an anxiety disorder.

So, people might have one panic attack and never experience another; others develop panic disorder as the result of becoming frightened of suffering another attack. Some sufferers then go on to experience constant high anxiety, phobias, and obsessions.

Regardless of your level of anxiety, the regularity of your panic attacks or the thoughts and symptoms you experience, I can tell you right now that you can and will eliminate them completely, regardless of what you may have been told before.

Remember: find a permanent solution, don't mask the cause

Drugs and psychotherapy are not the solution – they can provide temporary respite from your problem, but the only way to permanently eliminate high anxiety and panic attacks is to reverse the process that created them in the first place. In other words, you need to find the source of your stress, eliminate it, and start altering how you perceive 'stressful' situations.

The following techniques have all proved successful in helping people overcome panic attacks:

Face splash

Splashing your face with cold water at the onset of a panic attack activates the dive reflex. The dive reflex developed in humans to prevent drowning. It works by the brain slowing the heart rate and respiration in order to preserve oxygen levels in the lungs and blood at a time when it has no knowledge of how soon another breath can be taken. The heart rate can be effectively slowed using this technique.

Cold apple

Eating a cold apple slowly, or swilling cold water around the mouth, can also be an effective way to activate the dive reflex, in addition to using the mouth in a way that prevents the hyperventilation that exacerbates anxiety.

Remove and return

It is vital that you don't attempt to run away from your anxiety. The desire to remove yourself from a situation that is causing you to feel overly anxious is a normal and understandable response, but it's vitally important for you to understand that you can't run away from your emotions. Running away will only cause you to fear that specific situation more when you find yourself in it again. If you feel it necessary to remove yourself, PLEASE return to that situation. DON'T run away, run home, or hide from the situation. Go to a quiet place – the bathroom for example – splash your face with cold water, swill cold water around inside your mouth, take a slow, long breath and return to the situation. You'll feel proud of yourself when you have controlled your anxiety and warded off a panic attack. You'll also feel relieved that you haven't had to run and hide.

Panic attacks are horribly unpleasant – trust me I know. However, they are harmless and can be eliminated completely with the correct treatment.

Resources

I have helped tens of thousands of sufferers to eliminate panic attacks quickly and permanently by using The Linden Method. Our team of qualified anxiety, panic attack, OCD, and phobias specialists are available at any time to assist you in finding the fastest possible route to your recovery. The ultimate solution to panic attacks is multifaceted and requires a combination of knowledge, structure, reassurance, and support. But there are some things that can be done to minimize their impact. Visit www.thelindenmethod.com and allow us to help you.

Foundations for stress-free living

⊙ Anxiety is not a disorder or a disease, it is a natural response to danger. In order to eliminate panic attacks you need to reset your mind to respond appropriately at all times. The only way to do this is to convince your subconscious that it is safe. In order to eliminate anxiety and panic attacks completely, you will need to address the anxiety at its core using an anxiety elimination program such as The Linden Method.

- ⊙ To undermine and potentially stop a panic attack, use the tips mentioned above. With practice, these can be quite effective at removing the intense sensations experienced and deactivating the response.

- ⊙ Understand what panic attacks are, and the fact they are habit forming, which means if you usually avoid particular situations because you're worried you'll have a panic attack, stop avoiding them. Instead, enter the situation and if you start to feel anxious, do something to divert your attention: e.g. turn on your favorite music or sing or hum along to the radio, listen to a talking book or podcast, or go for a walk while listening to music or an audio book.

Day 9

SLEEP AND INSOMNIA

You know, you probably don't need as much sleep as you think you do in order to function efficiently during the day. The amount of sleep needed varies considerably from person to person: Winston Churchill, for example, was famous for only requiring five hours a night plus an afternoon nap. However, not getting enough sleep, whether it's due to insomnia (perhaps caused by worry or other issues) or poor sleep (due to noise or discomfort) quickly puts your mind and body under pressure, and over time sleep deprivation can cause a number of health issues as well as a decreased ability to handle stress.

How do you know if you're not getting the sleep you need?

Well, the biggest indicator of whether you're getting enough sleep is whether you feel refreshed when you wake. If you greet most mornings feeling heavy, lethargic, and tired, and this state worsens throughout the day, this could be because you are not sleeping long enough or that you are experiencing disturbed sleep. Long-term sleep deprivation may also cause the following issues:

- Mood swings
- Poor concentration
- Short-term memory loss
- Increased appetite
- Reduced motor skills
- Vision problems

In addition, tiredness can make people turn to stimulants (e.g. caffeine, sugary carbohydrates, or nicotine) to keep them going and, as we've already established, these simply mask tiredness temporarily and also affect your blood sugar and consequently your stress levels. So, if you're lacking sleep, it's important to find a 'real' solution. Fortunately there are many things you can do to promote healthy sleep, and there are a few simple techniques to help you to regain or maintain healthy sleep patterns.

- Create a healthy sleeping routine: go to bed at the same time every night and get up at the same time every morning.
- Drink a mug of warm chamomile tea 30 minutes before bedtime. You could replace this with warm milk if chamomile isn't your 'cup of tea.' Avoid sugary drinks promoted as sleep inducers, such as cocoa.
- Make sure you are comfortable in bed – bad sleeping posture is responsible for many cases of insomnia. If you ache when you get up, or suffer from neck or back pain, it

could be that your sleeping posture is an issue. Or maybe it's time to invest in a new mattress!

◉ Make the bedroom a place of rest and sex only. Put a sign on the door reminding others that this is 'your' space – this is particularly important if you have children in the house.

◉ Be sure to have a light snack 30 minutes before bedtime; going through the night without eating is a struggle for healthy people, and when you are anxious this becomes a bigger issue.

◉ If you lie in bed for more than 30 minutes trying to sleep, get up, make a drink of warm milk or chamomile tea, make yourself comfortable and snug on the sofa and turn on the TV at a low volume and watch until you fall asleep; no action movies though, just something semi-boring that won't hold your attention for too long.

◉ Breathing exercises can help you to relax and fall asleep. I've included two really useful exercises on Day 6 (see pages 51 and 52); make sure you do them every day.

◉ On the CD you'll find a 'Sleep' visualization that you may find helpful in combating insomnia.

Poor sleep can create many ailments, none particularly harmful, but all quite unpleasant. If you are uncomfortable in bed, if your bedroom is too cold or too warm, too noisy or even too messy or cramped, or just simply not a pleasurable place to be, your sleep patterns can be severely affected. What you wear in bed can also affect your sleep patterns – try wearing looser fitting garments or nothing at all, and see how this improves or worsens your sleep patterns.

Remember: focus on natural sleep

There are a number of sleep aids available on the market. However, I don't believe anyone should ever need to turn to medicinal intervention for insomnia. My clients have always found that insomnia drugs leave them feeling more tired the next day, so it is always best to exhaust all other options first.

A note to parents

If you're not a parent you can ignore this next bit, but if the most dearly beloved little people in your life are causing you to lose sleep on a regular basis, then read on. Most parents endure some sleepless nights – it's part of parenting – and it is usually worse in the first six months, or until your baby is sleeping though the night. However, long-term sleep deprivation really shouldn't be part of the deal. It can affect your ability to deal with stress, cause relationship problems, and make it more difficult to parent your child, so it's important to consider your own needs (and those of your partner) as well as your child's, and find a long-term solution to your child's sleep habits that works for all members of your family. This will probably take time, patience and, if you have a partner, a united method of helping your child create healthy sleepy habits. In the meantime, there are a few things you can do to get more sleep while you work on getting your child sleeping through the night:

- ⊙ If possible, work out a way that you (and your partner, if you have one) can get a couple of undisturbed nights' sleep a week – perhaps by taking turns to sleep in another room.

- ⊙ Have a relative or friend come over and look after your child for a few hours during the day (or even better overnight), so you both catch up on some sleep.

- If you're being woken up during the night, go to bed earlier than usual and rest as much as possible on your days off or when your child is napping.

- Whenever possible, take a nap during the day, or find somewhere to put your feet up and rest. You might want to keep a pillow and blanket in your car and take a nap on the backseat during your lunch hour. Most offices will also have a medical room that you can use to take a rest if necessary.

- If your child is sleeping with you and disturbing your sleep, it might be time to encourage them to start sleeping in their own bed.

- Don't be afraid to get some expert advice from your medical practitioner, health visitor, or a childcare expert in creating a happy, healthy sleep routine for your child – you are definitely not alone, and this time will pass.

Foundations for stress-free living

- Make your bedroom a haven of sleep and rest. This means banishing computers, TVs, phones, pets, and children, all of which can disturb the quality of your sleep.

- Caffeine is one of the worst offenders for causing poor sleep patterns. Firstly it is a stimulant, and one cup of coffee can stay in your system for several hours, and secondly it is mildly diuretic and so can cause unwanted trips to the bathroom in the middle of the night.

- Taking 30 minutes of low-impact physical activity every day will improve your quality of sleep, but avoid strenuous exercise (e.g. squash, running, or high-impact aerobics) within two or three hours of going to bed because these types of exercise cause an endorphin rush (also known as 'runner's high') and make it harder to wind down and sleep.

⊙ Have a light, non-sugary snack 30 minutes before you go to bed. Nighttime hunger can cause disturbed sleep as blood sugar levels fluctuate.

⊙ If you're worrying about a particular issue (financial or marital problems, etc.) and it is preventing you from getting to sleep or sleeping soundly, then help is at hand because we'll be covering lots of these issues in the coming days.

Day 10

ENVIRONMENT AND BEHAVIOR

Did you know that your reaction to your environment and behavior is one of the most important factors in the formation and perpetuation of high anxiety, stress, and worry? It is the 'software' that feeds your 'hard drive' (your brain) with the information it requires to 'reset' at a higher benchmark level in your mind.

You know which things in your life are positive influences and which are negative, and the solution to gaining equilibrium is to implement a filtration process. In other words, you have a choice: whether you see the glass as half-empty or half-full; whether you see your kids' toys as being a messy eyesore or the abundance of entertainment you've provided; your boss's appraisal of your work as criticism or as a tool for change. The fact is, we only live once and we need to maximize the positive potential of everything around us to feel fulfilled. So removing negative behaviors and influences is key to our happiness and wellbeing, and to reprogramming the subconscious mind.

From the moment we are born, we begin a steep learning curve of behavior and knowledge outside our inbuilt instincts. Everything we perceive through our senses is registered and stored in our brains, and it waits there to be accessed again as required. All the time this is happening, our brains are building new neural pathways of learning which create and store our experiences of life, our behaviors, and our achievements.

If our environment is perceived as negative, our brains develop a life experience pathway around those experiences. Some people get caught up in their negative environment and become part of it; others rebel against it, developing their own, positive environments and experiences. It's like children who grow up in abusive, alcoholic, smoky environments – more often than not, they grow up to be just the same as their parents.

Positive thinking comes from the inside out

You know the saying 'you are what you eat'? Well that is true to an extent, but what is more relevant is that 'you are what you think.' Some of the world's greatest scientists theorize that the Earth and everything in it is comprised of vibrating energy particles, This means that we are all part of a whole – all energy – and at one with the world, and that every molecule in our bodies is shared with everything else in existence. By 'thinking' positively, we can affect our own psychology and physiology and these thoughts will influence everything and everybody around us.

 Remember: take control of your thoughts
The power of positive thinking WILL affect your environment, the people around you, and the quality and enjoyment of all your life experiences.

You have the power to take control of how you interact with the world. I have a friend who never stops being jolly. People love to be around him because his enjoyment and pleasure in life is infectious and he never comes across as sickly or over the top in his pleasure. This person's life isn't perfect, but he makes every moment of every day count. He has few regrets, very few actual problems, and has a very fulfilled and happy outlook that rubs off on everyone he meets.

Positive thinking comes from the inside out – meaning how you talk to and about yourself makes all the difference. If you spend your days berating yourself with negative thought chatter such as 'Why do bad things always happen to me,' 'I am worthless,' 'No one listens to me,' and so on you are creating that reality each and every day you live.

If you want to check in with the quality of your internal dialogue, try this simple exercise over the next few days. Start by becoming more aware of your 'thoughts' about the following areas of your life:

- Money
- Relationships (partner, family, colleagues, etc.)
- Career
- Yourself

Keep a note of your predominant thoughts and start to examine where and how these beliefs formed for you. By focusing on how you talk to and about yourself, you may find that you are actually echoing values and beliefs of a parent, teacher, or other key influencer from your childhood. Once you've established your current thinking, ask yourself:

- Are these beliefs, judgments, or values true?

- How could I upgrade my thoughts to make them more positive?

- What thoughts are outdated, and how does my experience prove or disprove them?

The law of attraction

The law of attraction states that 'like attracts like.' In other words, positivity attracts positivity and negativity attracts negativity, so by manipulating your thoughts you can control the resultant outcomes. While there are arguments about whether this law can really exist, and how the science behind the theory works, it does seem that in many cases simply shifting your mindset means more positive outcomes come to fruition.

My wife and I laugh about our regular 'parking game' in which, on arriving at a parking lot, we visualize immediately finding a parking place in the area where we wish to park, and on most occasions, I won't say always, we do get to park there. Similarly, my mother nearly always wins the raffle when she attends charity events. When I say nearly always, I mean that I don't remember a time when she didn't win. Okay, these aren't big wins, but for decades she has been coming home late at night carrying a bottle of wine, a voucher for a free meal for two, or a signed print. I asked her why she thought this was happening to her and her answer was simple: 'It's happened so often now that I go almost knowing that I will leave with something.'

I believe that my mother's optimism is due to a series of chance wins at the onset that have created a deep psychological understanding in her that event equals prize.

While there is no supporting evidence or science behind the law of attraction, it does seem that some people attract positivity and some don't. And if you want a more down-to-earth explanation it may be that when you are positive and look for the good everywhere, then you are more likely to spot opportunities and feel more confident about taking them. Similarly, if you feel happy and have a sense of wellbeing then you reflect that feeling into your relationships and other people tend to mirror what they see back to you.

My conclusion is that adopting a positive attitude can affect your interaction with the world and other people, and if the feedback from those people and that environment is positive, your senses detect that positivity and the emotional response to positivity is generally positive. That physical and emotional response can develop into a habit of positivity as the mind creates new positive neural pathways.

As I recovered from my anxiety disorder and my life experience moved from stagnant and very negative indeed to fulfilling and positive, my mindset changed naturally as my world opened up, and I became more focused on those activities and experiences that created good emotional responses. This is, in effect, the law of attraction at work.

Try shifting your mindset and see what changes you experience. Feeling and looking happy are certainly a strong step toward changing how you feel.

Resources

If you haven't done so already, read M. Scott Peck's The Road Less Traveled. *This book provides expert yet gentle guidance in how to find a higher level of self-understanding. You may also find other books in the same series, including* Further Along the Road Less Traveled, *enlightening and useful in the quest for creating a more fulfilling and positive outlook.*

The law of attraction is also a recognized concept that has been around for hundreds of years. There are a number of books on the subject, including The Secret *by Rhonda Byrne, and a movie of the same name.* The Secret *is actually a series of devices that can influence the positive outcome of our lives. It is rumored that Oprah Winfrey is just one of the many successful advocates who use the ideas and techniques to guide them. The law of attraction is powerful and measurable, and it has certainly helped me in my life.*

Foundations for stress-free living

- ⊙ You control your internal environment, so stop battering your self-esteem and telling yourself life is hopeless. If you're lacking self-confidence, start by listing your positive attributes and put your focus on what you do like rather than what you don't.

- ⊙ In the same way, it is better to focus on what you do have rather than what you don't. You can become aware of the abundance in your life by starting a gratitude list. Include anything and everything that makes you grateful: for example, the sun shone today, my bus came on time, the guy at the grocery store smiled at me, the flowers in the park are in full bloom, and so on. Read through your list every day, add to it, and watch it get longer as the weeks pass. There is always something to be grateful for; you just have to be open to perceiving it.

⊙ Just as you can control the quality of how you talk to yourself, you can control what information you feed yourself from the outside. Fill your environment with people who make you feel good, and information that inspires you: e.g. listen to uplifting music in the car, watch programs on TV that are entertaining and informative, read books that focus on the positive aspects of life. Be discerning in what you read and watch, and who you associate with – it's your choice.

⊙ Being positive doesn't mean being foolishly over-optimistic that everything will turn out okay, it means taking the time to understand how and why you have the 'perception' you do of certain things in your life. If your 'perceptions' are simply inbuilt reactions that you've inherited from other people, then it's time to start thinking about what *you* really think and whether the glass really is half-full or half-empty. It's about taking responsibility for how you perceive your environment, your behaviors, and yourself.

⊙ Investigate the law of attraction and make up your own mind about whether you could make it work in your life. After all, you have nothing to lose and everything to gain from it.

Day 11

MONEY AND STRESS

As you probably know, the trappings of modern life can seem very attractive: a nice car, a big house, trips to sunny climes, etc. – most people fall into the trap of being predictable, becoming victims of retail madness and living life for the things they can buy, rather than the ones they can't! We have all been there, spending too much money on things that give us ten minutes of enjoyment and then quickly casting them aside for the next big idea!

Possessing nice things is addictive; it's a kind of drug, and the more you get the more you want. But there's an upper limit, usually set by financial constraints and sometimes by lack of vision. Very few people run out of things to buy when money is no object. But why do they need these things? Why are they so important to them? Most people would say that it's because they have something missing in their lives; maybe it is, but I say, most of the time it's simply the force of habit fuelled by the 'buying buzz' it gives us!

We make a conscious decision to either live to work or work to live, and the trappings of either can be suffocating, because once you get on that bandwagon, it's hard to get off. But it doesn't have to cause you stress and worry.

It is difficult to balance work and happiness, there is no doubt; however, it is also possible to have enough control over your finances to focus on other more important aspects of your life.

If financial troubles are causing you stress and worry then the best way to tackle this problem is head on, because ignorance is not bliss and understanding your finances and what you can afford puts you in control.

CASE HISTORY *Jason, aged 38, business owner*

Jason lost his job and couldn't afford his mortgage payments, so when his home was repossessed, his wife and children moved in with his mother-in-law. But there wasn't enough room for him, so he stayed in a local hostel. The situation was diabolical, and not only did he suffer with anxiety and stress symptoms, but his eldest child, Sophie, started being sick at school and was eventually diagnosed with separation anxiety.

Jason's mother-in-law contacted us regarding his anxiety and money worries. Over a three-week period, Jason's anxiety reduced, he became more focused on the matters in hand and, with help from our staff, he devised a life and financial plan. It was approaching Christmas and Jason and his brother-in-law started a Christmas tree business to make some fast money.

Now, two years later, they have a prospering farm shop and nursery supplying turf and Christmas trees. Jason was able to take back control of his finances by creating a structured approach, becoming passionate about a business idea, and systematically addressing each issue logically, without a sense of impending doom. Emma, Jason's wife, now also works in the business, making fresh cakes and cookies that she packages for sale and serves in the farm shop café, which she runs with help from her mother.

Take control of your spending

Start by making a list of all your outgoings, BUT at the top of the page put your total monthly income after tax. Write the necessities in red ink and the luxuries in blue, and at the end of the list add all your outgoings together to create a total. Take this total from your income and that should tell you how much you have left after all your expenditure. If this figure is equal to your income, or if you are spending money on credit cards, this could have the potential to add to your stress and worry. If that isn't the case, you may simply need to tidy up your personal cash accounting, making sure that you fall within this range every month and even allowing you to save a little, just in case.

Having a firm hand on your finances is incredibly important, as financial concerns account for more headaches than most other stressors. Most of us live beyond or at least to our means! This is a recipe for disaster.

You may not be the best money manager in the world; you may be a spendthrift, you may not earn enough money for your lifestyle, but you must get a handle on this before you add to your worries.

At work, I use an accountancy program to keep control of all my business income and expenditure; at home I use a great product that is basically a cut-down version of the same product. I suggest that you buy some software (although a pad of paper and a pen will suffice) and start taking control of your finances immediately... it's just one headache less to think about every month.

🦋 **Remember: you must take control of your spending**
I KNOW it's boring, I know it's tedious, and I know it may take 30 minutes a month to do... but if your finances are causing you concern, you MUST do this before it converts from 'worry' to 'nightmare'!

Foundations for stress-free living

⊙ If you're spending more than your monthly income and unsure where the money is going, keep a daily log of what you spend. You may find that your salary is disappearing on incidentals (e.g. cups of coffee, newspapers, etc.) that you don't really need.

⊙ Overspending on expensive gifts, trinkets, and gadgets can often be a sign of low self-esteem, especially if you can't afford them. If this sounds familiar, perhaps it's time to rein in your spending and realize that love (particularly self-love) can't be bought.

⊙ If you find you just can't resist those must-have purchases when you're out shopping, then leave your credit cards at home and just take enough cash to buy what you set out for – that way you can't be tempted by the bargain rail or to buy more than you need.

◉ When your spending has spiraled out of control and you're unsure how to pay off the debts you've accrued, it's time to get help from an independent financial specialist (the citizens advice bureau is a good place to start). Most financial institutions (mortgage lenders, credit card companies, etc.) will want to help you find a way to pay off your debts by coming to a payment agreement. Whatever you do, don't hide from your debts, but do stop spending.

◉ Some people find it hard to enter a store without buying something. If this sounds familiar, perhaps it's time to find a more rewarding outlet for your creativity. Start thinking carefully about what you'd love to do in your free time (e.g. painting, reading, hiking, or skateboarding) and make that your outlet instead. See also Day 29 (pages 187–191).

 # Day 12

RELATIONSHIPS

Relationships can be rewarding, amazing, and fulfilling, but on the other hand, they can be destructive, dangerous, and frightening! I am not just referring to romantic encounters, but family ones, too.

Under any circumstances, you need to decide exactly what your relationships bring to you, whether they are fulfilling, and how they could be improved.

You control who you associate with, and it is up to you and you alone to decide how you can minimize the negative relationships, maximize the positive ones, and mend the broken ones. If a relationship is good, it still needs to be nurtured; every relationship, including friendships, go through bad times, but it is up to you to make sure that the bad times don't last.

CASE HISTORY *Karen, aged 44, accountant*

Karen and her husband David had both been married before and been together for ten years, however, due to previous experiences, Karen described their relationship as officious and superficial at best. It was more like a business partnership than a marriage. Under the advice of her medical practitioner, Karen started taking antidepressants and very soon her physical health began to decline. David and Karen never communicated openly; they never made time for romance or intimacy, and hardly ever went on a date, or had days out or trips away together. David knew that something had to change and he had already been talking to his male friends about his concerns surrounding a second divorce, something he wanted to avoid at any cost.

During a conversation about her insomnia, Karen told one of our counselors about her home situation, and within minutes she was in possession of the list that you'll find below, which she studied, understood, and started to implement immediately. Karen called two days later to report that she and David had booked a trip away and had made love on two consecutive nights... why? Because she had asked him out on a date night, had dressed up for the occasion, and had given him no choice. In a couple of days, David had fallen in love again and the two were able to restart their relationship afresh.

The 29 steps to maintaining healthy relationships

Here is my list of 29 points to bear in mind. I am sure that you and I could sit down and write a list of thousands of relationship tips, but these are the ones that seem to work for me and have produced positive feedback from clients:

1 Try to pay more attention to what your partner says and do so more often. STOP talking and listen more.

2 Be prepared to do something that makes the other person happy on a regular basis! Go that extra mile to make them KNOW that you care.

3 If you aren't honest and open about your feelings, you are living a lie! Omission is lying, too! Speak openly about issues that could affect your relationship, because suppressing those thoughts and emotions can create a time bomb.

4 Laugh, smile, giggle, and have more fun.

5 Try to pull people into your enjoyment. If you find something that makes you happy, share it!

6 Be able to live your lives independently of shared responsibilities. Find common ground in joint activities, not in the chores of life.

7 Stand by your partner through thick and thin. Understand that relationships aren't all about fun and games; they are about trouble shooting when the hard times come along.

8 Find out what it is that makes you happy or sad, and try to focus on the happy things; this will have a domino effect on your partner.

9 The art of interacting successfully with others relies on your ability to listen to them. Be interested in what others find interesting, and if you are not, pretend to be!

10 Be impulsive: buy flowers, a surprise gift, a meal out, or take your partner a cup of coffee in bed… it works wonders! BUT, vary the surprise, because lack of creativity means lack of care!

11 Decide on an activity that neither of you have done before and try it with enthusiasm.

12 Sometimes in life we have to do things that we don't like… sometimes it's for people we love and just because they want us to do them… that's fine!

13 Ask your partner what they want from you and listen to what they say. If you don't, you may never find out!

14 Try to project your consciousness onto someone else for a while. Try to imagine what it must be like to live your partner or friend's life. See things from their perspective; it may inspire you.

15 STOP BEING NEGATIVE!

16 Follow through on every promise. If you don't, you will become known as untrustworthy and disloyal.

17 Being late means that you couldn't be bothered to prepare well enough to be on time for your loved one or you just didn't care.

18 Make sure that financial issues don't inhibit your relationship.

19 Be helpful and supportive – offer your assistance as often as you can.

20 NEVER get personal when you have a disagreement. NEVER criticize anyone's family.

21 Make it clear how important your loved ones are to you.

22 Don't ever lie. You'll get found out, and when you do, it will look really, really bad!

23 Anger has its roots in sadness. Look carefully at what angers you and find out whether it is YOU or the other person who is to blame, or whether you are just reacting to your own sadness.

24 Be considerate. Think through the consequences of what you do BEFORE you do it, because it's hard to reverse once you have carried it through.

25 If you disagree, please be sure that you are right. If there is any doubt at all, end the debate and find out the truth before re-entering into a discussion.

26 Relationships are about investments not bankruptcy. If you take too much out, you'll collapse the bank! Pay in constantly, even in small amounts, and the relationship will thrive.

27 Relationships are processes NOT events; they continue and mutate more than any other entity on Earth. They are a learning curve and an experience in one.

28 A relationship is about balance in every way. If the balance is off, the relationship will be difficult to weather. When a status quo is reached, the relationship will thrive.

29 THERE IS NOTHING WRONG WITH MARRIAGE GUIDANCE COUNSELLING!

I hope this list will help you to see that there are many things you can start to do today that will make a big difference to the people you love.

It is all too easy to become lax, bored, or complacent about your relationships... sometimes I hear my friends say, 'I just can't be bothered any more'... what a bad attitude. If they honestly can't be bothered, they seriously need some help!

Resources

Take a look at How to Win Friends and Influence People *by Dale Carnegie; I strongly recommend it to anyone who wants to improve every kind of relationship – it helped me enormously.*

Foundations for stress-free living

- Share your stress and anxiety with your partner (whatever its source); this is particularly necessary if you've been hiding your stress but your partner's noticed a change in you. He or she may not really understand the source of your feelings and may be taking your low mood or anxiety personally.

- Keep your bedroom as a place of rest, sex, and sleep only; don't take arguments or disagreements to bed with you.

- If you have children, remember that your relationship with your partner needs energy and resources too. Spend quality time together every day (not talking about the children), and if necessary retreat to the garden or the bedroom. Regularly book a babysitter and go out on dates together and, if finances allow, the odd weekend alone won't hurt either.

- Bad day at work? Row with a friend or family member? Whatever happens in your day, try not to bring it home with you and take out your frustrations on those people you love most. Leave the problem where it is (wherever it is) and make your home a sanctuary of love and peace.

- All relationships experience times of strife and difficulty, and if you want to keep the relationship intact hold the fact you 'want to stay together' at the foremost of your mind and understand that shouting matches and hurtful comments don't resolve anything, and may be very difficult to 'unsay' later.

- Look through the list of '29 steps to maintaining healthy relationships' again, but this time choose six or seven points that resonate with you (and preferably your partner) and make these the golden rules for your relationship. Then write them out, post them on the refrigerator (or anywhere in prominent view), and stick to them.

 # Day 13

AVOIDING CONFRONTATION

Confrontation is probably the largest cause of elevated anxiety. It can take many forms: confronting a boss, a relative, a partner, confronting a sudden truth, discovering a secret or hearing shocking news, witnessing a traumatic event – the list is endless.

Confrontation usually causes anger and sadness, and it is common knowledge that sadness causes anger in many cases. As anger and sadness rise, so too does the level of adrenalin in your blood stream, which causes a flood of anxious emotions, thoughts, and symptoms.

Ways to avoid confrontation

Avoiding confrontation is simple; here are my tips for coping with and avoiding it:

- Remove yourself geographically from the person or situation that causes it.

- Count to ten silently and regulate your breathing… slow, rhythmic, equal breaths.

◉ Go to a place where you can calm down without interruptions.

◉ Prevent exposure to the person or situation that caused the confrontation.

◉ Decide how best to cope with or deal with the confrontation while away from the situation. Return to the situation ONLY when you have decided on the best course of action.

◉ Decide whether you will benefit from the person or situation long term, or whether you are just treading water.

◉ If you require assistance, seek out a mediator, psychologist, counselor, or legal professional in order to help you rationalize your decisions.

🦋 Remember: who benefits?

The only person who benefits from your anger is your opponent; every time you become emotional in these situations you are reinforcing your anxiety and perpetuating how you feel.

It's important to understand that YOU hold all the cards: YOU can choose to stay or to go, to react or not. It is difficult, but, if you can turn the other cheek, you will win out every time.

Situations that leave you feeling drained are not healthy for you long term; be decisive about what you are prepared to tolerate, even if it means making sacrifices.

Please consider this carefully: it is surprising how many of us suffer under confrontation and don't realize it. It can dramatically increase your stress and anxiety levels, but removing it from your life can create an intense feeling of relief and wellbeing.

Foundations for stress-free living

- ◉ Take some time to examine the sources of confrontation in your life. What or who makes you angry, sad, or anxious. If the same old arguments keep cropping up again and again, perhaps it's time to forgive and let go, find another way of doing things, or simply avoid that person in future.

- ◉ If your life is filled with confrontation and anger, it's often a sign of low self-esteem or lack of confidence. Whatever its cause, a shift toward more positive ways of thinking will help you resolve your inner conflict. See also Day 10 (pages 75–81).

- ◉ What you eat is fundamental to your mood. Stick to my healthy eating suggestions and make sure you're getting good-quality vitamins and minerals from your food and including sources of tryptophan, which the body requires to make serotonin. See also Day 1 (pages 1–19).

- ◉ If you find that the confrontation happens after you've had a few drinks then stop drinking. In situations, or people, that cause you stress you need to stay clear-headed and focused. See also Day 3 (pages 25–29).

- ◉ Keep updating your gratitude list (see page 80), because remembering all the good things and supportive people in your life will boost your self-esteem and keep you feeling positive.

- ◉ Physical or mental abuse is not acceptable in the home or workplace. My only advice in this situation is to leave the situation immediately and seek help from the most appropriate person (e.g. human resources, the authorities, or a trained counselor).

Day 14

AVOIDING POWER SAPPERS

You might ask: 'Who or what are power sappers?'

Power sappers are people who draw energy from you, but give nothing in return. These people bring nothing but negativity to the party; they suck your energy, your vitality, your drive, and your ambition. Power sappers can be anyone in your immediate vicinity and they usually prey on easy targets. It might be tough to acknowledge this to yourself, but sometimes power sappers can be those closest to you: your partner, your child or parent, a friend, or a work colleague.

Power sappers are indiscriminate, because they use anyone to empower themselves. Like vampires they suck other people's life force from them in order to boost their own self-confidence (if you can call it that in such circumstances). Sometimes they do this by undermining you; sometimes they do it by bettering you and then drawing your attention to it; sometimes they just make your life miserable by projecting their emotional baggage and problems onto you.

Dealing with power sappers

It is vital, not only for your mental health but also for your future goals and ambitions, that you minimize contact with power sappers. If possible avoid them at all times; they do not positively contribute to your life and serve no purpose. IF they are people who you can't avoid, such as your child, boss, or a work colleague, simply shut down your emotions when in their presence and do not allow them to influence your anxiety or mood; they sap your power to build their own and have no respect for you and your wellbeing. You'll be surprised by how quickly they'll realize they are not 'getting' through to you and find someone else to 'sap' instead.

You need to be structured in your decisions about which people are your power sappers, so make a list and try to identify exactly what each of these people bring to you. If you don't, ask yourself this about the people you know:

1   Do they ever volunteer anything to you for no personal gain?

2   Do they make you feel sad, uncomfortable, or fed up?

3   Do they ever bring anything positive to your life in any way?

4   Could you rely on them in a crisis?

The answers to these four simple questions can be difficult to answer, especially when they address issues with people with whom you should feel close. However, they can be very revealing.

So, what do you do once you have identified these 'rogue friends'? You minimize contact with them, you devise methods to undermine their negativity, you bring them into environments where they cannot openly undermine you without ridicule… in other words, you stop their behavior in its tracks before it gets you down.

I know this sounds simple, and that in reality it's much more difficult, but it is vital that you stop the power sappers. Let them self-destruct instead of destroying you.

 Remember: find some power givers

Surround yourself with power givers. You know who they are – they are the people who feel good about themselves and make you feel good about yourself; they empower you, inspire you, and make you feel positive about all you do or want to do with your life.

Foundations for stress-free living

- ◉ Knowing your values is more than just a code of ethics and moral practices; it's also about being able to know immediately whether your or another person's behaviors or actions measure up to 'values' that you have chosen. People who know their values usually have high self-esteem, feel confident about who they are, and are less likely to be a victim of power sappers. Re-evaluate your values and codes of behavior, know your values intimately, and then live by them. It just makes life simpler.

- ◉ If you maintain a busy, structured life the power sappers will find it harder to find you and you'll find it easier to escape because you'll be busy doing your own thing. See also Day 22 (pages 143–149).

- ◉ Don't share your goals and ambitions with people that you don't trust; they'll just put you down. Instead, search out the people who'll encourage you and share your plans with them. That sounds obvious, but just because you like or even love a person it doesn't necessarily mean that's where you'll find a buddy to share your dreams.

⦿ If you have no choice but to get into a conversation with a power sapper (this is particularly true in the case of family members that you can't avoid), focus on your breath, keep a smile on your face, listen without becoming involved in the conversation, and keep your own plans and thoughts to yourself. Don't worry, they'll soon get bored and find someone else to sap.

⦿ Unwanted phone calls from phone sappers can also drain your reserves. If possible, screen your calls, but if you end up on the phone with a known power sapper, set a time (say five minutes) for the conversation and politely end the call when the time's up.

⦿ Keep doing the visualizations on the CD – they will help you to feel more relaxed and boost your self-esteem.

Day 15

BALANCE, CHALLENGES, ENJOYMENT, AND MEANING

Today, let's talk a bit about balance. Balance… what does that mean?

Balance, or equilibrium, is when time spent at work, with family, and on personal fulfillment are in the ratio that most fits your circumstances. BUT, more importantly, this ratio must mean that none of the three factors are compromised in any way. Think of them as being like a triangle. You should aim to give all three focuses of your life approximately the same amount of time.

Balance your commitments to suit your circumstances

If any of these three factors become compromised, this may not affect you directly, but it may affect those you work with or care about. In turn, they may begin to suffer with stress or anxiety, become unhappy about their relationship with you, become angry, sad, confrontational, or depressed, which will affect you in the long run.

Let me give you an example.

Danny is married with three young children. He works in the city as a sales agent five days a week. He leaves home at 6 a.m. and usually returns at around 7 p.m., just as the children are going to bed. While his wife, Gilly, gets the kids tucked in, Danny eats his evening meal. Once the kids are asleep, Gilly does the dishes and tidies up after the day, while Danny reads his emails, plays a little poker, and falls asleep on the sofa. Danny plays golf most weekends – just a few rounds with his friends. Once a week he pops out for a drink or two and sometimes goes for a meal on the way home. Gilly stays at home and looks after the children; she can't afford to have a hobby as money is allocated to other things. Gilly's day is usually spent cleaning, tidying, preparing clothes and packed lunches, collecting and dropping off and occasionally she stops for a cup of tea with her friends. The family usually takes a two-week vacation somewhere cheap and cheerful, but occasionally they have a package trip abroad for a week. Although the children are quite well behaved for Gilly, they act up when Dad is around, and consequently Danny complains he has to be the disciplinarian. He blames Gilly for being too 'soft' on them, and this causes a few disagreements on parenting styles. Gilly used to play racket ball regularly, but she is now too tired and unfit to play.

The butterfly effect

Okay, you get the picture? I don't think I need to say any more about this family; the imbalances are obvious, and this is what I call 'the butterfly effect.' The butterfly effect is actually a theory of quantum mechanics which basically says that a butterfly flapping its wings in South America will affect the weather in Central Europe, say. Okay, it's an extreme concept, but one with a deep scientific basis. Similarly, what we do, even things we perceive as the trivia or 'norm' of our everyday lives, CAN have a dramatic domino effect; they can affect others in ways that we don't even perceive, and may even be directly detrimental to our lives without us even realizing it!

But the question is, what do you do about it? Danny works hard for long hours, but so does Gilly. The kids hardly get to see their dad during the week, and at weekends he plays golf. Gilly misses him, but Danny can't stand the kids arguing and screaming all the time.

The answer is in balance. Danny can't stay at home, because he needs to earn money, but when he gets home, instead of heading straight to the microwave, he could set 15 minutes aside to read to his children; that way they have contact with their dad and three people are happier already. When the kids are in bed, Danny could eat his dinner and he and Gilly could spend some time discussing their day before they snuggle up on the sofa to watch their favorite show (the dishes and tidying could wait until the morning). On weekends, Danny could play golf in the late afternoon so that the kids don't feel deserted on a Saturday morning. Instead, the family could visit friends or go on an outing, just to create some family time and a definite break from the working week that the kids can look forward to. Danny could see his friends every other week and the couple could book a babysitter and go out together for dinner and spend time together. As a result of spending more time with their dad, the children are less likely to misbehave when he is around.

 Remember: create structure

The watchword here is structure. It's easy to fall into bad habits that mean all family members have little to look forward to. With variety, regular time with your partner, your children or family, and a sensible working life, things become so much simpler.

Creating balance with structure

Reassess the structure of your week. Be honest about who or what benefits from your time at all times. It might be helpful to try to see what you do from other people's perspective; it may be that what you do works for you, but not for others. Be aware that when others are not happy, this can come around full circle and bite you on the butt in other ways. A subtle change to these habits can cause dramatic changes, which create greater flow in your life and the lives of those you care about.

Importantly, the old routines will become memories – you will all be happier and so will the people around you.

Here are the questions I ask clients to ask themselves to identify and eliminate the things they do that could be changed for the better:

⊙ Does my work life require modification?

⊙ Can my work life be made more effective?

- If my work life is as ordered as it can be, who does it affect and in what way?
- How can I soften the impact of my work life on those around me?
- Who benefits from the time I am not working?
- How can I maximize the benefits for those I love during the time I am not working?
- What can I do to make those I care about KNOW how much I love them?
- How can I spend more time with my partner doing the things we used to love to do together?
- Do my hobbies mean that others experience any loss of 'down time' in their routines or enjoyment?
- What do all of these modifications bring to me?

If you answer all of these questions truthfully, you will find that there are changes you can make that will dramatically alter your enjoyment of life, and undermine any stress you experience.

Foundations for stress-free living

- There is a famous saying that's worth remembering as you bring more structure to your family and working life: 'love is spelled T.I.M.E.' You can never get back that time with your loved ones: children grow up, family members age, loving couples can grow apart – feed your most precious relationships with time and they'll repay you tenfold.

- Personal time for you is also important. Although you may find it difficult to plan long periods of personal fulfillment time, you should include some every day – whether it's spent on your hobby, getting some exercise, or just sitting in the garden with a cup of tea.

⊙ Whatever mode you're in – work, personal, or family time – be present. In other words, don't spend that time taking sly peeks at your emails, thinking about what to cook for dinner, or being distracted by the thoughts in your head. Give the person you're with (even if it's just yourself) the benefit of quality time where you focus on what is happening now. We'll be talking more about mindfulness and being present tomorrow.

⊙ Create healthy, stable routines in your daily life: sit down with your partner for dinner (or if you have small children aim for twice a week at least); spend time in an activity with your partner and/or children every week (for example, a game of soccer at the park, a movie, dinner out); create special one-on-one time for each member of your immediate family every week – write it on the calendar and then follow through with your promise.

⊙ Time management is vital, and if you feel like life is a constant battle to keep up with everything then it's time to take a long hard look at your commitments and reprioritize what's not important. Simplify your life. Think what can wait until tomorrow, what doesn't need to be done; what things can you just let go of to make more time for the things that need your attention? See also Day 22 (pages 143–149).

Day 16

THE PAST, PRESENT, AND FUTURE OF YOU

You have experienced the past, and you can influence the future by the actions you take today, but the only real time is happening in the present – the NOW. This is your present experience and it is unaffected by the past or future.

Memory has a purpose; it's a filing system for your experiences, both negative and positive. Negative memories – past failures, regrets, and things that didn't work out the way you planned – need to be filed away in the archives of your mind, allowing you the opportunity to create positive memories that can then become your focus.

It is so easy to dwell on the bad things that happen to you, and some can be very bad... life is full of pitfalls and sadness. However, those who navigate it successfully are able to identify and file those experiences efficiently in the library of their minds, then move on and enjoy the present as it is happening.

We can do nothing about the things that happen without direct input from us – they are the concern of others or 'fate' itself, if you believe in fate.

The things that we can influence are those things that should most concern us, and it can be our job to positively or negatively influence those things if we so choose. The path is ours to take, we just need to be decisive and move forward.

Stay in the present

Live for today, not yesterday, and make this moment the first moment of the rest of your life. That doesn't mean you shouldn't have goals or plan for the future, but it does mean being aware that your life is happening right now. If you spend your life worrying about the past or the future, you put yourself into stress mode because you can't influence the past or future by fretting about 'what ifs,' 'maybes,' or all the possible outcomes. Stress doesn't exist right now, so focus on the present.

You may have heard of the term 'present mindfulness.' This simply means focusing on what is happening now. So whatever activity you're doing – whether it's watching TV, working to meet a deadline, playing with your children, eating dinner alone – focus on that activity. The show you are watching, your thoughts about your work, the laughter and expression on the faces of your kids, or the taste of the food. In this way you don't allow your mind scope for worrying about the past – which you can't change – or the future, in which anything could happen. So, just focus on the present, and when you need to plan for the future (to book flight tickets, create a business plan, or set your goals, etc.) be mindful of that activity and don't think about the TV show you watched last night, the deadline you missed this morning, and what you are going to eat for dinner. In other words, whatever you're doing, be present.

Hanging on to the past

The fact is that those who hang on to the past rarely experience a positive future.

When I moved back to the UK from Germany in 1992, I walked into my local pub to find the same people standing in the same places, talking about the same things they had done years previously. However, there was a marked difference; they only talked about the past, they rarely spoke of their goals or ambitions and they were pretty scathing about mine!

I was shocked that they didn't seem to have moved on; they even recounted stories of what we did previously, even more than ten years earlier! I can't remember most of what they talked about because so much has happened in between, but because their experiences are limited, they harp on about the same old stuff!

If you find that you are constantly talking or thinking about the past, it might be time to find a way to literally put it behind you. Whatever is holding you back can usually be resolved by using the following three-step plan:

Accept

Bad things happen; some are terrible, life-threatening, self-esteem-destroying events that seem impossible to accept.

However, they happened and you can't undo the past; you cannot change events, you can only accept them. Instead, think:

⊙ What positive lessons did I learn from that experience?

⊙ What negative lessons did I learn from that experience?

If, because of that experience, you have developed negative behaviors (become fearful of loss for example, or distrusting) understand that this was your way of coping with the event at the time. Accept what has happened to you, but acknowledge that you won't let it influence your present any longer.

Forgive

Difficult I know, but forgiving wrongs and, perhaps more importantly, forgiving yourself, is necessary if you want to move on with your life. It is difficult to forgive the perpetrators, but in doing so you actually free yourself of their influence on your life. They hurt you in the past, but by hanging on to past wrongs you are actually allowing them to continue to hurt you in the present. Forgive everyone and everything.

Move on

Give your energy to the positive, life-enhancing people and things in your life and let the negative, bad memories go. If you find your mind straying back to the past then acknowledge the thoughts, but don't follow them back into the bad old days. The less attention you give old memories today, the less they will bother you in the future.

 Remember: start afresh
Each day is filled with fresh possibilities and new opportunities; this is the first day of the new you... make it count!

Foundations for stress-free living

- When you feel anxiety and stress beginning to build, take a moment to bring your mind back to the present moment and your breath. Breathe deeply and focus on the present and what is happening now.

- Being present is also the purpose of meditation. You don't have to learn to meditate, you can just practice stilling your thoughts by bringing your mind to your present activity: whether it's washing the dishes, talking to a colleague, or writing a report. Simply focus on the task in hand.

- Ensure that you make time for some low-impact exercise every day. Tai chi and yoga are both excellent for teaching present-mindfulness and helping bring calmness into the rest of your day. See also Day 7 (pages 55–59).

- Avoid being dragged into past events by other people. Remember, you don't have to get involved in their dramas, regrets, and old memories. Focus on creating great new memories today.

- Find safety in the healthy routines you've created – your diet, lifestyle, relationships, thinking, and home life – and if your mind keeps turning over old events and behaviors that are holding you back, distract yourself with activity. In this way you stop old patterns of thinking from taking over your attention and learn new, healthier behaviors.

 # Day 17

GOAL SETTING

Yesterday we discussed the importance of not being dragged back into the past and staying in the present, but it is also important to be clear about where you're heading, because your actions today really do create your future. So today we're going to think about goals.

Your goals can be anything that's important to you – personal, business, or financial – anything that will bring you happiness and contentment.

Create your goals

The basic principal of goal setting is simple.

Take a blank sheet of paper and write down your short, medium, and long-term goals. Be realistic about your ability, but stretch your expectations so that the goals are challenging for you.

Never be disappointed by not achieving your goals; instead, be impressed by your ability to chase them.

Try everything; take every opportunity that arises and regret nothing – it's all part of the challenges and your personal enjoyment of life.

1. Be able to make decisions

Being successful comes from being able to make the decision to make that goal happen by what you do, and not by chance, luck, or good fortune! Only YOU can plan and execute success.

2. Stay focused

Keep your eye on the ball – it's a moving target so don't take your eye off it! Your ability to remain focused has a direct effect on your success.

3. Do you know what failure is?

It's one of the outcomes of having 'tried', and it's part of the road to success! However, if you don't utilize the lessons learned by failure, it will be time and resources wasted.

4. List your goals

Make a list of your goals and stick to them. You may think you are Mrs. or Mr. Memory, but you can't remember everything.

5. Make plans

Remember the five Ps: Proper Planning Prevents Poor Performance – one of the main rules in successful business and life strategies. Write a list of actions against each of your goals to bring it closer. Divide the actions into easily manageable tasks and put an approximate date against each one.

6. Delegate and question

No one knows everything, so ask questions, collect knowledge, and don't be afraid to ask for help. Where your goals involve your partner or family (e.g. moving house) delegate tasks that involve the family. If your goals are to expand your business or some other venture, get help to bring your plans to fruition.

7. Get off your backside!

If you just sit around and wait for the success bus, you'll see it pass by quickly and you won't be able to jump on. You need to action the tasks on your list one by one. In this way the future begins to take care of itself.

8. Be kind to yourself.

Throw yourself a 'Scooby snack' every time you enjoy success, complete a task, or see your goal taking shape. Even self-awarded rewards are empowering.

9. Don't let the side down – even when the side consists of just you!

You are your team. Don't allow anyone to influence your goals, ambitions, and work ethic. Share your plans and dreams with enthusiastic and helpful friends and ignore any naysayers.

Resources

Now, here's my hot tip for goal-setting skills. I really suggest you read The Ten Commandments of Goal Setting *by goal setting and life skills expert Gary Ryan Blair, also known as The Goals Guy®, who is one of the top strategic thinkers in the world. An author, speaker, coach, and consultant, he is dedicated to helping his clients win by creating focused, goal-directed lives. His book includes vital information, including a self-study learning guide; how to be decisive; how to focus on results; how to write down your goals; planning essentials; auctioning your goals; follow-though strategies; commitment and personal integrity and a lot more.*

Foundations for stress-free living

⊙ Review your goals regularly and do something to bring them into fruition each day – even if it's simply planning your next move.

⊙ Write them down somewhere safe: in a notebook, or on your computer, as well as posting them somewhere visible, such as the refrigerator door or on your desktop.

⊙ Don't discuss your plans with negative naysayers (even if they are close family members); instead, share your plans with those people who will encourage you and give you advice when you need it.

⊙ Creating a goal doesn't necessarily need to have a financial gain, it could be a personal accomplishment such as to get fit, give up smoking, climb Kilimanjaro, spend more time away from work and with your loved ones, or on your hobbies. You can achieve anything you want if you have a plan and then follow through with actions.

⊙ Be positive about the future. It is unwritten, which means that anything is possible provided you spend some time planning and taking action to create your desired outcome. To help you on your quest, I've included an 'Empowerment' visualization on the CD; use it daily to manifest your goals.

 # Day 18

WORK TIME AND YOU TIME

So what are 'YOU time' and 'work time'? Here's the lowdown. If you don't know how much time you spend in each area of your life, how do you know when you have balance in your life? If you just go through life feeling constantly harassed by work and other commitments, what time are you actually investing in YOU?

YOU time is fundamental to living stress fee. This is your time to recharge, do the things that make you happy, and plan for the future. So from today, I'd like you to selfishly claim a section of each day, say one hour, to do things for you. You could have your nails done, have a massage, lie down and dream, or simply read a book – the choice is yours.

YOU time is when you remove yourself from interruptions, from noise or stress, and make that time yours, every day. Ask a friend or partner to assist you with this if need be; it's the only link you have with the old you, pre-children, pre-work, pre-marriage... it's your 'grass roots' time.

Putting it in simple terms, our lives are made up of three elements: work, sleep, and leisure. Many people feel that their lives consist of too much work, not enough rest and sleep, and very little leisure – does this ring a bell?

CASE HISTORY *Stuart, aged 31, broker*

Stuart worked as a broker in New York. He was originally from Perth, Australia, and his NY family consisted of three tropical fish and a Columbian housekeeper. Torturous work schedules and life practices born of focusing on work, finance, and success meant that Stuart had spent the previous seven Christmases working in the city, alone. But this year was different. His mother had been unwell earlier in the year, but due to his obsession with work and a boss who would, despite Stuart's money-earning capabilities, fire him if he went back to Perth, Stuart hadn't returned home.

He woke up one night sweating, crying, and feeling overwhelmed, and knew that change had to happen. Stuart could feel physiological changes developing within him. At just 31 years of age he was suffering from insomnia, IBS (irritable bowel syndrome), and migraines, and he knew that if he didn't take action, his condition would worsen. For the first time in his life, he felt vulnerable and desperate. Taking advice from one of our life coaches after finding The Linden Method on the internet, Stuart started to restructure his day, where possible making time, even if only a few minutes, to use the techniques and devices recommended in this chapter (and the rest of the book). Within days, Stuart was feeling much better and his demeanor significantly improved, which also had a domino effect on his work, as his productivity dramatically increased. On December 22nd, his boss presented him with his Christmas bonus check and in the envelope there was also a first-class airline ticket to Perth.

Creating time for YOU

There exists a way of assisting yourself to redress the imbalance by regaining an equilibrium in your work life. This is called a 'personal timeline,' and here's how to construct one.

First, draw a straight, horizontal line on a piece of paper. Make the line about 15cm (6in) long. This line is your 'day line,' representing a 24-hour period, so break it down into six equal parts: each section represents a four-hour period.

Now decide how much sleep, on average, you require each night: if this is eight hours, mark in an eight-hour period on your timeline, so this equals two four-hour sections.

Now do exactly the same thing for the amount of time you work each day. Then also mark your travel time to and from work on the timeline.

By this point you'll be able to plainly see that the remaining area on your timeline is your YOU time, your playtime – the time that you can spend doing whatever you wish.

Now, I understand that most people have children, partners, family members, and commitments to mark onto the timeline, but for now at least let's presume that you have four hours per day for leisure activities.

Now this is how the timeline chart will help you:

1 Ensure that your work time doesn't run outside the 'work' area of your timeline: if it does, ever, make moves to redress this imbalance. Work should never be allowed to over-run into leisure time.

2 Gradually work toward reducing your work time block so that you can enjoy more YOU time.

The lessons that you can learn from this kind of exercise are important, and include:

◉ Learning to combine your activities. Using your physical and mental self leads to more fulfilling activities and a greater learning experience.

◉ Letting go of your 'life habits' and rituals: e.g. checking your email when you should be focusing on home activities.

◉ Being more spontaneous. When you know what makes you happy then you'll be more likely to recognize or plan activities that equal YOU time.

◉ Learning to refuse when others make unreasonable demands on your time. Saying 'no' to the stuff that you don't want to do is important, because it eats away at the time you could be spending doing the things that make you happy.

◉ Recognizing when you've over-committed yourself to helping other people, and taking steps to redress the balance.

🦋 **Remember: make time for you**
Successful management of your personal timeline will result in you making more time for you and doing the things that make you happy.

Ask yourselves these questions:

⊙ Is this the best use of my time?

⊙ Am I going about this task in the right way?

⊙ If I stopped doing this, what would the outcome be?

Be honest about the answers and I think you will be quite surprised.

If you want more control over your life and more time for you, this technique can help to make all that a reality. The only additional skills you require for making this work are discipline and patience, but it will pay dividends.

Foundations for stress-free living

⊙ Don't waste your work time by getting involved in office politics, checking in with social media sites, and so on. Examine your working habits carefully. If you're wasting your working time and having to work longer hours to make up the time, you are eating into your YOU time which will bring you greater dividends.

⊙ When you leave work (whether you work 50 miles from your office or at home), close the door to work mentally and physically. At the end of the day, spend five minutes reviewing the day and a further five minutes planning tomorrow, and then leave. You might want to include a little ritual such as tidying your desk or clearing up your workspace. Once you have left work, close the door on it – physically and mentally, and don't check in with email, torment yourself with the latest office politics on your journey home, or worry about what you still have to do tomorrow.

- If you have a commute home, fill that time with things that give you enjoyment.

- Finances may be an issue, but do make use of labor-saving devices where you can to make more YOU time: for example, shop online for household items to save unnecessary trips to the store; invest in a dishwasher (if you haven't already); consider using a laundry service or getting some help with domestic chores; if you always work outside the home, investigate the possibility of working from home once a week or a couple of times a month to save yourself that commute.

- Look out for exercise classes that you can take in your lunch break, or use your time to walk around the park, visit museums, browse the bookshop, or read a book. Use your time wisely and this can be YOU time, too.

- If you have instituted an exercise routine that you enjoy, have started planning for your future, and resolved home issues, then creating more YOU time should already have happened. Keep reviewing how you spend your time and don't allow yourself to slip back into old habits.

 # Day 19

DISASTER OR OPPORTUNITY?

First, let me tell you this: JUST COPING IS NOT AN OPTION!

If you are just coping, it means that there are still unresolved issues to address.

It is vital that after a trauma, no matter how insignificant the trauma may seem to others, to learn how to THRIVE. The experience of thriving means that the traumatic experience has absolutely no detrimental effect on the sufferer's life.

Okay, memories may exist, they always will; however, it is vital that they are rendered as such and stored appropriately in order to minimize their impact in other areas of life. Like the bereavement process, painful memories should be allowed to weaken by using techniques described on Day 16 (see pages 111–115) and below, which will help the healing process to take place. If the sufferer is constantly fed reminders of the painful experience, it is doubtful whether they will ever be able to move on and thrive.

Coping with trauma

The most effective techniques for coping with painful traumatic events involve a structured timetable of activities that not only creates focus and diversion, but also builds on and embellishes your life experiences in order for you to find fulfillment and happiness powered by the painful experience and the newfound hope you pull from it.

We all experience negativity in life – it's part of being alive – but what survivors do is use the negative force to find new life energy.

When I recovered from my anxiety disorder, I previously made the decision that living my life in painful, frustrating limbo just wasn't good enough. I told myself that IF I was going to stay like this forever and then drop dead, I might as well do something in the meantime – no matter how scared I was… and I was pretty scared, believe me.

Through the chest pains, dizziness, horrible thoughts, panic attacks, stomach problems, and many other awful complaints, I decided that I would get up, get dressed, go out, and challenge myself to take the best photographs that I possibly could. It was this that tipped the scales for me on my road to recovery.

Of course, simply taking a few snapshots can't eliminate an anxiety disorder, but it was a major factor in my recovery, that's for sure.

You have a choice

You can decide to allow your negative experiences to overwhelm you, and be the guiding force for the remainder of your life, or you can decide to create success from disaster and drive yourself forward; it really is your choice. Will you be a victim or a success? It is your choice – 100 percent.

If you reject the challenges of life and give in, you can only rest assured that YOU and only YOU have put yourself there. It's all too easy to play victim, but from the outside you look weak and from the inside you feel it! Don't sit around waiting for something to happen, or for someone else to pick you up and dust you down, because chances are, it won't happen. NO ONE ELSE LOSES OUT... that I promise you, no matter how sorry you feel for yourself, I guarantee no one else feels as sorry!

Make that choice today. Create energy from your experiences and drive forward. You will become a hero and everyone around you will look up to you as a winner, a guiding strength and an inspiration. Instead of someone who simply GAVE UP!

Often, out of trauma, loss, and sadness, new opportunities are born!

By focusing on fulfillment and what makes you feel happy – by becoming emotionally involved with a new activity, a new initiative, or simply a new hobby – you can experience that distracting emotion that fills us when we fall in love with something or someone. It's all about emotion. How we respond to our environment and the people around us emotionally is the 'decision-making' process that creates the 'snowballing' that compels us to continue with that activity or experience. When something feels good, we tend to do it more. From survival of the human species to getting married, from career, hobby, music, and food choices to favorite vacation destinations, our subconscious psychology provides us with an internal review system that focuses us on and moves us toward those things that keep us safe and provide us with a simple and happy experience of the world around us.

It is this internal mechanism that provides the positive energy that will fuel your ultimate fulfillment and turn disaster into opportunity when it is required.

Resources

I recently read a book by Robin Sharma that I enjoyed immensely. Called The Monk Who Sold His Ferrari, *it's a wonderful tale of how a rich, overweight New York lawyer turned his life around after having a heart attack in a courtroom. His transformation was miraculous, and the lasting peace and happiness he found was incredible. Read it; it really is an amazing story of triumph over adversity.*

Foundations for stress-free living

⊙ Dealing with trauma – whatever its cause – is about acceptance. Accepting that desperate situations such as divorce, death, loss, and illness are as much a part of life as love, birth, health, and wellbeing. You can't have the good times without the bad. The fact is that life is full of polarities – good/evil, rich/poor, overfed/starving, and one is not possible without the other. Accept that the event has happened, but avoid dwelling on it by keeping busy. The quicker you move on with your life the quicker life will return to normal.

- ◉ Be kind to yourself as you overcome the difficult times: speak to yourself gently, treat yourself to plenty of YOU time, and focus on creating healthy eating, working, exercising, and sleeping patterns.

- ◉ Don't be afraid to seek professional help from a counselor or therapist who can help you come to terms with your current situation. Sometimes, talking things through with someone with an 'outside' viewpoint can really help put things into perspective for you, and it usually only takes one or two sessions to find a resolution.

- ◉ Using the ideas in this program means you should have already created more structure in your life, and this will help you cope with traumatic experiences.

 # Day 20

CONFIDENCE

Regardless of your ability or achievements, have confidence in the decisions you make and take responsibility for the consequences.

Be able to apologize for wrong decisions and prepared to adapt to changes. Confidence comes from not fearing the outcome of your actions. Only you can take control of this, but if you do, you will be able to do and say things that are usually the preserve of super-achievers.

CASE HISTORY *James, aged 52, local government worker*

James came to us suffering with chronic anxiety and panic attacks. He was dyslexic and had under-achieved at school, despite having an enormous intellectual resource. He left school with low grades and followed his father into a local government job as a refuse collector. James had been married, but his dismissive attitude to work, coupled with his constantly changing moods, became intolerable for his wife, who had left him and remarried several years previously. James now lived alone and had limited access to his children. He would work as many hours as possible and call in at the pub on his way home from work every night. Afterward he would pick up takeout and eat it in front of the TV. James had never considered having another relationship, and his mood was so low and his anxiety so high that considering change in any aspect of his life seemed impossible to him. He was existing, but not living.

James's sister introduced him to us and he was skeptical at the outset. He believed he was too old and too set in his ways to be helped, but we soon proved him wrong. He completed The Linden Method and his anxiety receded quickly, his confidence improved significantly, and he started doing much more. James joined a sports club and learned boxing. By month two he was feeling healthier and stronger, and had developed a confidence in his ability to learn and better himself. We introduced him to a dyslexia education program, which we've referred many people to, and very soon he was reading more and excited at being able to keep a diary without struggling or becoming frustrated. Now James is doing a distance-learning degree in psychology, he is managing the department at work, and he has a girlfriend. The only thing holding James back was his own belief in his creative intellect, and what that resource could produce when utilized effectively.

Confident living

Here are my rules for increasing your confidence.

1. Focus on positive outcomes

The biggest problem with having confidence is overcoming the 'what if' question. The 'what if' question undermines our confidence as it creates fear – fear of the consequences.

'What if I try this building project myself?' Well, the house could blow up! This negative train of thought is common in those who lack confidence, because they are focusing on the worst possible scenario. People who have confidence are fully aware that there could be negative consequences; it's just that they only focus on the positive ones! It's about changing your mindset and NOT fearing the outcome. KNOW WHY? Because everything can be put right!

2. Boost your confidence

IF you haven't done something before and you are lacking confidence, you can do two things to give yourself a confidence boost right away. You can give it a 'trial run' and you can use 'role play.' By practicing what it is you have to do, even driving to the place and running through the activities you have to do, you minimize your anxiety by familiarizing yourself with it before you have to do it 'for real.'

Role-playing with someone you trust really helps, too. It doesn't matter what the situation is, simply pretend that you are in it and try to 'live it' as best as you possibly can. This really works. Visualizing yourself in the situation can work equally well. Just ensure you make your visualizations as bright and positive as possible, as this trains your brain to expect a positive outcome.

3. Look outside yourself for answers

I have a saying – in fact, I have two: first 'don't reinvent the wheel,' and second 'stand on the shoulders of giants.'

Why start from scratch when you can replicate what others have done? It doesn't make sense to create and test, change and retest until you get it right if someone has already done all the testing for you! Very few things are NEW; someone has usually done them before and that being the case, copy them.

There are so many successful role models out there in the world. Instead of trying to beat them, use their success to fuel your own! Think, if they can do it, so can I.

4. Fake it until you make it

We are what we do (not just what we eat and think!). In other words, our behavior makes us who we are. If you act timid and weak, you will be timid and weak instinctively. If you 'act' strong and confident, even though you may not feel it at first, you will become confident and strong. From now on you are not YOU, you are Brad Pitt or Angelina Jolie PLAYING THE PART OF a more confident YOU! Do you understand? You are now an actor being a confident you, and very soon that behavior will become part of you!

5. Be objective

Make sure that your perspective of the situation you're facing is realistic and justified. Try to see it from someone else's point of view. Ask yourself, would they cope in the same way or do the same things? If you can look at the situation objectively and be honest with yourself, things are usually much better than they first seem.

6. Don't belittle yourself to others

Don't be a 'yes' person. Ask for what you want and need in a respectful and intelligent manner and you will usually get it!

7. Don't let your most dangerous adversary be you

You know that internal dialogue you have with yourself every time you are faced with adversity? The one that says things such as, 'you can't do that,' 'you'll fail,' or 'it'll never work.' From this point forward, please IGNORE IT! If you can't ignore it, try to imagine it speaking in Donald Duck's voice or Bugs Bunny's. Suddenly it becomes a lot more difficult to take seriously, and it's much easier to just tune it out.

If you use the 'Confidence' visualization on the CD and consistently implement the rules given above, you'll find that your confidence will grow and you'll stay focused.

Resources

You may have heard of Anthony Robbins, the amazing US life coach. His CD program Inner Strength *is highly recommended for helping build confidence and self-esteem – many of our clients have found it life changing in helping them to access their confidence.*

Foundations for stress-free living

◉ Starting any venture by imagining the worst-case scenario will drain your confidence. Be positive about what you can achieve.

◉ We'll be talking more about posture on Day 27 (see pages 175–181), but how you stand affects how you feel and how others perceive you, so make sure you walk tall and purposefully; smiling will also help you feel more relaxed, confident, and at ease, even if you don't always feel it.

◉ Keep your self-talk upbeat, light, and positive. Don't allow your internal nag to get the better of you. Remember, the past has gone and each moment, hour, and day can be a new beginning.

◉ Be smart and use your YOU time in ways that give you confidence: be with people who make you laugh, do activities that make you feel relaxed and grounded, tune out the naysayers, and say 'no' to anything you don't want to do.

◉ As you start taking positive action toward achieving your goals, write a list of your successes (however small) each day: for example, I had a really good conversation with my boss today and he listened, or I cooked a delicious meal tonight. In this way, you build your self-esteem and confidence by proving how you are achieving success each and every day. Reminding yourself of things you do well builds confidence and self-esteem.

 # Day 21

FEELING FULFILLED

Feeling fulfilled is the key to happiness, to stress-free living, and to finding enjoyment in each and every day.

Feeling fulfilled is the result of a combination of realistic goal setting, the removal of stressful influences, and personal achievement; in fact, every positive influence you can gather on your journey.

Feeling fulfilled is simpler than you think: it requires a little planning, but, apart from that, as long as you have conviction for your need for personal success – regardless of how that success manifests itself (business, sport, money, family, etc.) – you shouldn't go far wrong.

So, what can you identify in your life that could potentially make you feel fulfilled?

◉ Career success?

◉ Money?

◉ Sporting achievements?

- ◉ Relationships?

- ◉ Children/family?

- ◉ Travel?

- ◉ Educational achievements?

- ◉ Language abilities?

Path to fulfillment

Write a list of what YOU need to achieve for YOU. This should NOT be a list of the things you need to do for others, although this might also create a feeling of achievement for you and so, if it does, add it to the list.

Be realistic about what you can achieve, but don't underestimate your abilities. So, if your wish is to be a deep-sea diver that might work out, but if your wish is to visit the *Titanic* without the aid of a diving bell, then it's probably best to rethink. In other words, know your limitations and push them!

Feeling fulfilled could be easier than you think. Take some time alone. Go to a quiet place, perhaps the park or the beach. Find a comfortable spot to sit, and then close your eyes. Take a deep breath in and picture yourself happy and contented doing what your imagination tells you would make you feel fulfilled. Make a note of what you see. Repeat this exercise to discover the true you – the 'you' that is free to do all the things that you need to do FOR YOU.

It may be that you discover things you want to do that might upset others, or might not 'fit in' with their plans. You then have a decision to make: to drop the idea, to go through with it and ignore the consequences, or to compromise in some way. There is usually a solution if there is conflict.

I can only suggest things to guide you to this ultimate state of fulfillment. There is no 'magic wand' that can award you fulfillment, as you have to attain it yourself.

I hope that this might have sparked inspiration in you and that soon you will be seeing your successes in your mind's eye and making plans to see them through.

Resources

Using the 'Empowerment' visualization on the CD accompanying this book will help you to find the things that bring you fulfillment.

Foundations for stress-free living

- Many people believe that simply having more money will bring them fulfillment. However, research shows that those with substantial amounts of money (particularly those who have inherited or have suddenly gained wealth through a jackpot win) are as happy (or not) as those who struggle to make ends meet each month. You hold the answers to your happiness, the knowledge about the things that make you happy.

- Make sure you write your plans down and review them regularly. Don't list them and then immediately forget them. Write an action list of what you need to do in order to make each one come true for you.

◉ Be happy at other people's success. Remember the law of attraction from Day 10 (see pages 78–79)? Celebrate their success and see it as evidence that change happens all the time. Feel positive that you will achieve the things you desire.

◉ Before you go to sleep each night, spend five minutes reviewing your day – what has brought you fulfillment? In this way you acknowledge your successes each day and increase your quota of positivity.

 # Day 22

GET ORGANIZED

Organization is key to living a stress-free life. If you allow your life to become a tangled mess of string, tightly bound up and almost impossible to unravel, you are asking for a disaster to happen.

My father always said to me, 'Make a list.' He was right, making a list of all that you need to achieve in a day or week or month is probably the most important stress-busting tool at your disposal. It teaches you to focus on priorities and execute your tasks in an organized and structured way each day. Nothing is more effective for organizing your time, and striking through your completed tasks is very satisfying!

Break down problems into manageable tasks

If you are confronting a problem made up of multiple elements, break it down into its parts and ask the same five questions about each part of the problem. Note down the answers on a sheet of paper for reference later.

1   Identify the problem EXACTLY. Define the problem accurately and objectively without ambiguity. Be mindful of the fact that emotions can give a distorted view and make some tasks seem like insurmountable problems.

2   What has caused or created the problem to arise? List what you perceive as the catalyst for the problem. List as much detail as possible about the current issue and why and how it has arisen.

3   What could the solution be? Brainstorm a list of solutions, but do this quickly, spontaneously. Now, quickly, off the top of your head, write down between five and ten potential solutions. Now study the list and prioritize and number each item in order of importance.

4   What course of action can you now follow in order to solve this problem? List every source of help, every resource, and every approach you need to solve this problem efficiently and then make a strong decision about how much time you will need to resolve it.

5   Identify your ultimate goal. What are you hoping will be the outcome? What would be your ideal solution and how would this end up? Also, ask yourself whether your problem is worth the investment or whether it would be better to abandon it and look for a better solution; it may be that the problem isn't worth solving.

By truthfully addressing these five questions, you will be able to structure a results-focused solution for every problem you encounter, no matter what the scale. Instead of 'troubleshooting,' you will be able to calmly take on any problem and conquer it with confidence, avoiding the sometimes inevitable stress and worry it can cause.

Don't be a slave to problems; they are just an opportunity to use these five questions from now on. By tackling each problem rather than ignoring it, you create a sense of achievement and increase the number of opportunities that are available to you. For example, you may be unhappy at work and it is creating stress throughout your life. Tackling the problem using these five questions and then taking the course of action you've decided may mean you need to resolve your current issues at work by finding another job, talking honestly with your boss, or retraining in another career. Yes, it will require some effort and planning, but resolving the issue will bring you confidence and happiness, and free you from that nagging stress that has invaded your life.

Resources

If you find that making lists leaves you a little cold, then you might want to try a mind map instead. Developed by Tony Buzan in the 1960s to help him study, mind maps have helped millions of people develop their creativity, improve their studies, and organize their work. Visit www.thinkbuzan.com to learn more about this groundbreaking technique and trial Buzan's mind map software.

Perfect Practical Planning (PPP)

This method allows you to itemize and prioritize activities in a structured way, enabling you to methodically work through goals set by you. Routine and planning are the two key words for organized, stress-free work and life practices, and implementing this structured approach will pay dividends.

It is important not only to plan future work, but also to intelligently analyze completed work. This method will allow you to do that effectively.

The 'PPP form' is a practical way to organize your work. Below is a simple illustration of the types of questions that you should include, but it is best to add and modify the questions to suit your individual needs. It is important that you limit the PPP form to one page in order to distil and focus on your objectives; otherwise it can become too messy and disorganized.

Allow yourself a small amount of time each week to look back at the previous week and to add to the plan for the following week.

The goal of this process is to save your precious work time, to focus your thoughts, and to put structure into your work practices.

Your ability to plan and structure your work routines improves with time. With the PPP method you can build a weekly picture of your life, your achievements and goals, and follow the development of your work practices and achievements. A simple one-page form or chart can consolidate your thoughts and provide a structured platform to cope with most tasks competently. Focus and structure are the keys to successful work practices. Try to be structured and exact with the questions on your form, as this will provide more targeted answers.

Use your form as the foundation on which to structure your working life. It can become the cornerstone to maintaining focus and poise, ultimately producing a fulfilling and stress-free working life.

Types of questions to include on your PPP form

1   What have this week's achievements been? What is the most outstanding achievement this week?

2   How have I progressed:

    A. Leads/sales?

    B. Production?

    C. Cash flow?

    D. Contacts?

    E. Ideas?

3   Have I responded to all enquiries and correspondents? Is everything up to date?

4   Is my work on target to meet objectives/goals/expectations?

5   List new contacts. List any future appointments set up.

6   Did I successfully achieve all that I could this week? What do I need to revisit/amend? What went well?

7   Did I eat well, exercise, and try to be healthy in my approach to work?

8   What's my priority list for next week?

9   Which people do I need support/help from next week? Have I prepared for and set up all meetings for next week?

10   Am I adhering to my priorities list?

11   Is this week's goal plan being adhered to and is it achievable?

12   Where or who are the potential pitfalls? List the solutions to these also.

13   What could I do to ensure that next week is as successful? Am I prepared?

Foundations for stress-free living

◉ Organizational skills are paramount to stress-free, structured life practices. If you ignore them you risk being subjected to chaos and negative outcomes.

◉ Creating healthy patterns in your work and home life will naturally bring more organization to your life. You don't have to be a slave to routine, but knowing what happens when brings a sense of safety and order to your life. See also Day 18 (pages 121–131).

◉ If your home, car, or workspace is cluttered and messy, get tidying and sorting. The general rule is to throw away, pass on to someone else, or sell anything that is no longer working, useful, or valuable to you – and that includes books you'll never read, clothes you'll never wear again, and broken gadgets and household items (honestly, they will never be useful). It may take a few days (or longer, depending on the level of clutter) to get everything sorted and tidied, but think how much time you'll create by being able to find just what you need, when you need it. Clearing the clutter is one of the most powerful stress-busting tools I know, because clearing your space helps you clear your mind. Try it, you might be surprised at how much better you feel.

◉ If you're sticking to my healthy eating plan and avoiding fast and processed foods (which contain nasty hidden sugars and bad fats), but finding it hard to find time to cook healthy meals each day, try this time-busting tip. Prepare double the quantity each time you cook a stew, soup, or other healthy dish. Eat some and freeze some. That way you'll always have a tasty, healthy meal in the freezer for next week.

◉ It is your choice, but I believe that if you adhere to the ground rules covered today, then your stress will fade away. Why? Because stress is a state of mind: pressure causes stress if you don't 'own' it. Make the decision today.

 # Day 23

CONSCIOUS CHOICES

You have a conscious choice to make when confronted with adversity: you can either decide to allow the problem to propagate, grow, and invade your life or, somehow, you can salvage an opportunity from the wreckage.

When you apply this principle to some of life's more serious catastrophes, it can seem a little mercenary. However, the people who move on, deal with and leave tragedy behind and make a success of their lives are also those who can take advantage of every pitfall.

On average, humans experience 25,000–50,000 unique thoughts per day. If 90 percent of those thoughts are negative, what effect will that have on your enjoyment of life? EXACTLY, you will end up depressed, disheartened, unfulfilled, and fed up!

Positive affirmation is commonly used to challenge negative beliefs and it works on the theory of 'you are what you think.' So, if you are able to take control of your thoughts and then, in turn, your actions, you can quickly become a 'positive thinker' and the domino effect through your life can be quite powerful.

Please don't confuse matters here though. I am talking about using positive thought to manipulate your responses, NOT to change your neurology.

Some cognitive therapies believe that by changing what you think, you can eradicate anxiety disorders, but that just isn't possible. If it were then simply upgrading your self-talk would stamp out anxiety disorders, and that's just nonsensical.

Making conscious choices

You don't need to change your FEELINGS to affect the way you think… it's easier than that and, in fact, the complete opposite. Here are some guidelines:

⊙ **Keep a note.** Keep a notepad nearby and write a list of all the negative thoughts you have during one day. This exercise will quickly make you aware of just how negative you are! I think you will be shocked. As you write each one down, think about how you could have perceived the event/thought differently, or how you could have shifted your viewpoint to produce a different outcome. Be aware of your 'opinions' as you keep this list, because opinions about yourself and others are vital to identifying your negative moods and their effect on your self-esteem and your trust/opinions of other people. You could make two columns in your notepad: in the first column write the 'negative thought' and in the second column write the alternative thought. This way you can quickly identify and keep tabs on how to amend your thought processes. Soon your behavior will change and the positive thoughts will outnumber the negative ones.

⦿ **STOP focusing on problems.** Problems are opportunities to apply your ability to find a solution. NO problem is too large, and it most likely that in a month's time you will have forgotten what the problem was!

⦿ **STOP CATASTROPHIZING!** IF you program yourself to focus on the worst-case scenario, regardless of the actual size of the problem, its effect on you will be maximized! Listen to the words you use; words such as NEVER, CAN'T, WON'T, ALWAYS, etc. NOTHING is black and white as there is always an area of gray from which to salvage some positives! Of course, if you are one of those people who thrive on being the victim, this advice won't help you – you have condemned yourself to a life of self-inflicted misery. That's not to say that you can't change that fact, but if you do, it's going to mean being very honest with yourself and most 'psychological self-masochists' won't do that!

⦿ **Get feedback.** Ask someone you trust to tell you whenever you are doing or saying something negative; you could even help each other. If this is someone you spend a lot of time with on a typical day, this could prove an excellent exercise for improving your environment, office relationships, friendships, and work productivity! A negative environment will generally produce negative results.

⦿ **Be positive.** Try this the next time someone asks, 'How are you?' Answer, 'Fantastic, thanks, and how about you?' Positive reinforcement does work – before long you will feel as good as you proclaim!

- ◉ **Make some changes.** When you have identified when, how, and about what you are being negative, focus on how you can change these things. It could be that definite events or people are the catalyst for this negativity, so you need to make decisions about how YOU can change your reaction to these in order to make you feel better. Be selfish about what you want and manipulate others and situations to get what you need from them by being positive and calm. Next time a catalyst appears, mentally knock it down and move on.

- ◉ **Stay focused.** A good reminder can be to wear a rubber band on your wrist. Every time something negative happens, twang it to remind yourself that you MUST react POSITIVELY!

If you implement the ideas outlined in this chapter, you will immediately start to see how a simple change in your thought patterns can have a very positive impact on your life.

Resources

Louise Hay has developed a number of powerful audio CDs that teach how to use positive affirmations to change your perception of the world. I give every guest on our Anxiety Recovery retreats a copy of Louise's 100 Power Thoughts CD. Louise is a world-famous life-development coach and the author of bestselling books including You Can Heal Your Life. Her books are wonderful, and her audio CD is so easy to listen to – it is inspirational and relaxing, and gives direct contact with her warm, reassuring voice as she reads out her own long list of positive affirmations.

Foundations for stress-free living

- You choose which role you play: survivor or victim, hero or villain, prince or pauper. Make sure you aren't playing out a role just because it's familiar, and that it isn't causing you unhappiness and stress.

- Spend more time just being present in the moment; time spent focussing on the activity in hand allows your brain to just relax and be present. See also Day 16 (pages 111–115).

- Keep your internal and external environments pristine and positive. Don't trawl the newspapers or the internet for bad news if it makes you unhappy; don't get into conversations with people who like to moan and groan; and don't waste your time talking down to yourself. Instead, watch, listen, and read information that inspires you; spend more time with the positive happy people; and tell the nagging naysayer in your head to take a hike.

- If you take a happy and confident attitude, you'll find that it will also cause those around you to be happier and more confident. This is the law of attraction in action because people tend to mirror other people's emotions, so be a positive mirror. See also Day 10 (pages 75–81).

 # Day 24

COLLECT HAPPINESS

Are you aware that many accumulated small pleasures can create more happiness than one big one? Trust me, a constant stream of pleasure is a lot more satisfying than one large explosion of pleasure! This can be applied to so many things because, like all good things, pleasure usually builds slowly, and in fact most of the pleasure is in the 'build up.'

You can choose to go for the 'big finish' or to continue with the ongoing pleasure. The excitement of many of life's fulfilling experiences is in the build up, the preparation, the challenge, and most of the time the end result is over too quickly.

Planning your life around a constant flow of small pleasures can help you unlock a very positive mental attitude.

If your day is a stream of stress and chores, punctuated at the end with a sense of relief as your head hits the pillow, you are going to spend much of your day focusing on your bed! That's just not positive now, is it? It is all too easy to be swallowed up by circumstances, and to gain support from others by becoming dependent; it's human nature to go into 'self-preservation mode' when everything seems to be against you. However, with some simple guidance and support, it doesn't take long to learn how to collect happiness.

CASE HISTORY *Ann-Marie, aged 26, homemaker*

Ann-Marie was pregnant at 15 and married at 18. Her mother suggested that Ann-Marie contact us because she was growing increasingly concerned about her daughter's appearance and general demeanor – which had become increasingly somber in recent weeks – and she was concerned that Ann-Marie was developing a depressive condition. We quickly established that the problem was that Ann-Marie had never realized her potential; she had never pursued her dreams or even experienced the places she had desperately wanted to see as a child. She had lived in the same town her whole life, and had only left the area three times (and two of those occasions were school trips). She now had three children, and a husband who liked a drink or two. She looked sad, and despite attempts by her mother to give her a makeover and to pull her back into her 20s, Ann-Marie looked 50, acted 60, and felt 90.

It wasn't that her environment was unhappy, but more that she had forgotten how to SEE. She still LOOKED, but never with enough intent to see past her immediate environment. Although she wasn't having panic attacks, Ann-Marie was restricting her geographic movements and occasionally becoming a little distressed if her mother suggested a trip in the car, or a visit to the beach. It soon became apparent to our support staff that Ann-Marie had stopped collecting happiness. She had created an environment in which she existed but failed to LIVE effectively, and had dismissed the possibility of getting joy out of any of her daily tasks or experiences. Ann-Marie had switched off her positive emotions, used tactics such as head bowing, and adjusted her dress, her posture, and her interaction with people to control incoming sensory data. She was consciously rejecting positive emotions in order to protect herself.

In a few days we taught her how to SEE again; how to get those fast and fulfilling emotions flowing, and how to interact with people and places in order to flood her body with feel-good hormones. Ann-Marie learned that interacting with the world didn't have to mean opening herself up to responsibility and risk. She found she could remain in control, but also feel happy and fulfilled at the end of each day.

Plan your perfect day

By planning each day so it includes regular breaks, regular YOU time (as described on Day 18, pages 121–126), for fun things, listening to music, walking in the park, chatting to friends, etc. you can make your day much less tiresome, and more interesting and productive.

Remember when you were at school? Presuming you had some fun at school, regardless of the intensity of the learning element, you always looked forward to going to school so that you could show everyone your new toy, new hairstyle, discuss last night's

TV shows, play, and have fun. Of course the school day was filled with boring stuff; however, the glimmers and moments of fun in between made the whole thing bearable.

Now it's up to you to find out what makes you tick, identify things that could offer moments of relief, and make sure that you build them into your daily routine.

Start by evaluating your life on paper. Write down all the stuff you HAVE TO DO. Then write down how long those things take. Calculate how much spare time you get in among those chores, and how much time you have outside that time. Really study your timetable and discover what your life is truly all about.

 Remember: kids can make fun out of anything

Try being a big kid… it really works. Our adult lives are constructed from endless responsibility, chores, work, and structure, but think back to the last time you actually had real fun – fun that penetrated through the steel hull of your daily chores and infiltrated your life positively. Chances are, you don't remember the last time you felt that way. You have an opportunity to change all that.

You have a choice to make: live or survive?

Choose to live and that means balancing your necessary chores with your enjoyment of life! This IS NOT a dress rehearsal; one day it will be too late to change. THAT'S YOUR RESPONSIBILITY!

We have already talked about many of these ideas in the book, but if you want a distilled list, here are my top ten tips for creating happiness:

1 You don't need to start psychoanalyzing, investigating, or dissecting yourself or the past. Instead, look to the future: plan your daily schedule ahead of time, filling the holes with intellectually challenging activities.

2 Nourish yourself correctly in order to create physical equilibrium and healthy blood sugar levels. Remember also to drink fluids throughout the day at regular intervals. Choose foods and beverages that give you pleasure and make you feel good.

3 Look, don't just see. Be sure to really investigate everything you see fully, learning how to truly LOOK at everything that enters your environment. Looking at objects activates much deeper levels of the subconscious mind involved in building memory and learning, and produces much stronger emotional responses to those things. Think of how, when you were a child, you were able to spend ages studying the clouds, an ant, or a blade of grass, and use that way of seeing your environment as your role model.

4 Do something new. The brain will function like a train for much of the time – your autopilot only controlling tempo as your habitual behaviors keep you on track. By introducing new activities and interests, you stimulate the emotional center of the brain, activating the emotion of happiness.

5 Act positively. Act as if you love what you are doing. Act confidently. Act as if you are fully engaged with everything you do. Behavior changes thoughts. The more effectively and seamlessly you practice being the person you wish to be, the faster you will become that person.

6 Never reward yourself with things that have a negative impact on you. Many people reward themselves by binging on sugary or unhealthy foods, or with an alcohol-fuelled night on the town. The subconscious mind will create an anchor between the action and the damaging behavior. It is far more productive to reward yourself with walks, exercise, or a massage, for example.

7 Do something selfless for a friend or friends. Bake a cake, write a letter, hand-make a gift, have a tea party, organize a woodland walk – do something for someone or a group of people that you care about. Make it heartfelt and selfless. The positive feedback you get will affect the release of feel-good hormones.

8 Stop profanity and negative language. I call this the 'echo principle.' If you stand in a cave and shout profanities, they'll be thrown right back at you. People are like cave walls. You get back what you put out there, so stop.

9 Hug the people you love. Spend a little time each day being affectionate to your loved ones and the feedback you get will flood your body with feel-good hormones. Don't neglect anyone. It's so easy to be distracted by life issues and blinded by monotony.

10 Take a weekly break from the grind (get a babysitter if you have children) and go do something that steals you away from responsibility. Doing something different – something that represents a full departure from normal activities on that day at that time – is enough to activate feel-good hormones. Go on a 'date night' with your spouse; go out for a meal, or catch a movie, perhaps. Go to a friend's house and play games. Have a massage. It doesn't matter what you do, just DO IT and reap the benefits.

Foundations for stress-free living

- Take one of the ideas in my top ten list and put it to use today to find out how good it feels to create happiness.

- Stop focusing on what you don't have and keep thinking about what you do have by regularly reviewing and updating your gratitude list.

- Plan for and enjoy the big, happy events, like Christmas, vacations, and weekends away, but if you're squirrelling away all your funds to pay for the big events, even up the balance a bit and put some money aside for days out, treats, and fun activities throughout the year.

- Cherish every little success or happiness – in both yourself and in loved ones – it's amazing how simple things like a loving hug, a friendly phone call, or five minutes with a favorite book can bring you a sense of wellbeing. It's a case of being on the lookout for the things that make you happy.

- Find a way of making those must-do chores more fun: sing your way through washing the car or cleaning the kitchen floor; use your commute to work to listen to inspiring audios, learn a foreign language, or watch DVDs (if you're not driving); invite friends to meet up at a local bar or coffee shop for an impromptu get-together; take the kids to the park after school and play soccer or tennis with them; listen to a comedy radio show while you cook dinner and laugh while you rustle up a delicious and healthy meal.

# Day 25

DRAW ON YOUR STRENGTHS

When someone asks you what your strengths are, do you give out a little chuckle, become embarrassed and underestimate your abilities? If you don't, either you are confident in your abilities or you're masking your lack of confidence with a practiced script!

I asked this question of 40 applicants for a job recently, and most of them giggled, dipped their heads, and then lifted their eyes in search of a clever, inspirational answer.

It's not a difficult question, but most people struggle with it. Why? Because it's something most people don't consider… ever.

We all have weaknesses, but those who focus on them tend to use them as a benchmark; a point that should never be exceeded. Confidence is the main issue among these people, but lack of knowledge about the person they should know best is equally to blame in many cases.

Do you know what your weaknesses are? And do you know that, other than the extreme fears of life and physical constraints, you shouldn't actually have any! And any you do have should be made into reasons to compensate.

CASE HISTORY *Claire, aged 25, dance instructor*

A young woman called Claire came to see us because she had an eating disorder. When I first saw her I was quite shocked. Claire was very thin and she told me that she had gone from 140lbs (63.5kg) to about 95lbs (43kg). She was eating very little indeed, and had stopped eating in public completely. Claire was chronically anxious, felt nauseous all day, made herself sick daily, and was having up to six panic attacks every day. Claire worked in a call center and hated her job. She told me that she was a classically trained ballet dancer and had previously taught at a ballet school in South Wales, but when the school closed she had grabbed the first job she could find, and for the past two years had worked in the call center with a friend from school. Claire told me that she had never been confident, and that she knew she would probably stay at the call center now, make it into a career, and move up through the ranks.

Claire had lost sight of her passion. She had resigned herself to the fact that she would lead a restricted life, that her anxiety would dominate every decision, and that those decisions would condemn her to a life half lived. I wouldn't accept that, and I didn't want her to either; it was unacceptable in the truest sense of the word. All that held her back was her lack of belief in her abilities.

She was happier to buy into her perceived weaknesses than to acknowledge her strengths and use them.

I worked with Claire on a life plan – a timetable based on her own desires and strengths – of the life she would have IF she were someone else, someone stronger and more capable. Then I proved to her just how strong she was by drawing on her past accomplishments, by asking her to dance for me, by asking her about her knowledge, her skills, and her awards.

Within an hour, Claire was starting to experience the positive emotions she once took for granted and, as I dragged her into an existence in which she was strong and capable, her mind responded by secreting the hormones associated with positivity, excitement, and joy. On day two, Claire went into Cardiff with her mother and ate a full curry with all the trimmings. One week later, she handed in her notice at the call center and started her own ballet school. She gained weight, she gained confidence, and she gained self-respect, and it all started with a one-hour conversation in which I showed her how to ignore her perceived weaknesses and draw on her true strength. She never returned to the eating disorder clinic.

Take every opportunity

After I had recovered from my anxiety issues, I reached a point when I said to myself: 'You've been through the worst, it can't get any harder than that, now it's all uphill and you have to take EVERY opportunity that life feeds to you.'

This was a serious turning point for me. I decided that if I was going to find my ultimate happiness and fulfillment, I had to experience as much as possible – to fill my life with new challenges and learn new skills.

I started by accepting every opportunity that came along, starting with: 'Charles, can you do anything about this broken chair?' Without thinking about it, I'd say, 'yes,' knowing full well that I hadn't got a clue about where to start… but I would learn!

I accepted every challenge and it paid off. I found my ultimate happiness and I am living it right now. That doesn't mean I said 'yes' to the power sappers (see pages 101–104) or to the things I knew would drain my energy and reserves. I simply said 'yes' to the challenges that I would have been too scared to tackle previously. In other words, I trusted myself to succeed.

My son Charlie has a condition called Duane's Syndrome in his left eye. His vision in that eye is about 5 percent and the other eye is very short-sighted indeed. So, you'd think his ball skills would be bad, his hand-to-eye coordination would be affected, and he would fall and trip regularly? NOPE! A soccer talent scout has spotted him, he is top of his class at gymnastics, and I can't remember the last time he fell over. He is five years old!

What is the story to be learned from my amazing child and people like Claire? Triumph over adversity; use what you've got to its full potential; focus on your abilities, and build on all of these things. You are the master of your destiny, and so you decide what you need to do.

So I ask you: what are your weaknesses?

(Subtle clue to answer: 'I have none.')

Resources

I read a great book called Starting Over: 25 Rules When You've Bottomed Out, *by Mary Lee Gannon about her experiences in overcoming challenges, which I highly recommend. At 36, Mary was a mother with four young children and a self-employed husband when she found herself in divorce litigation and then homeless. Seven years later, she was president and CEO of a large foundation. Mary's encouraging writing and interactive approach offer both inspiration and strategies for overcoming setbacks in business and in life. It's a great read.*

Another wonderful book is Discover Your Inner Strength, *a collection of growth strategies from four of the world's leading experts – Jim Bandrowski, Stephen Covey, Ken Blanchard, and Brian Tracy.*

Foundations for stress-free living

- ◉ There are lots of inspirational stories about people who turned their greatest weakness into a strength, or overcame huge adversity. Pick up some movies or books and get inspired, and don't forget to keep using the 'Empowerment' visualization on the CD.

- ◉ If you were told as a child that you were 'bad' at something, or that 'you'd never learn' – e.g. the piano or mathematics – and it's always jarred with you, then challenge yourself to become a master at it. I guarantee that you'll surprise yourself by how much talent you actually have, and how much pleasure you can gain from showing yourself that you can do it.

- If you set yourself a challenge every week and then complete it, your confidence and self-esteem will quickly grow.

- Allow your attitude to spread to your partner, colleagues, friends, family, and children. Be positive about them and for them. In this way, you create a mutually nurturing environment.

 # Day 26

BEAUTY, WHERE IS IT?

When was the last time you felt invigorated and awestruck by something beautiful?

It's probably been a while. We tend to get so caught up in the trappings of modern life that the simple pleasures fall by the wayside. But it doesn't matter where you live or what your surroundings are like, you can find beauty everywhere... and I mean everywhere.

Open up to beauty

The eyes are the most sensitive organ for capturing emotion. Sure, it's nice to be touched, or to smell or eat something good, but ultimately, seeing something good arouses immediate thoughts and sensations... some pleasurable and others not so!

We are blindfolded by life. Our routines mean that all we perceive isn't all we see. We see beauty everywhere, but it is so filtered out and overwhelmed by the focus of everything that we have to do each day that we hold on to drudgery.

When I was recovering from my anxiety disorders, I bought a camera and it turned out to be the best move I ever made! It wasn't expensive: just a standard film camera with a zoom lens. It made such a difference to my recovery that I now recommend photography to all my anxious clients.

WHY?

Have you ever looked through a viewfinder? What does it do? It makes you focus on a slice of the world. Then it makes you select the most attractive shot possible.

Try it. Go out into nature and find the most beautiful shot possible.

The very action of focusing your consciousness through one eye into a confined area (the frame) has the effect of diverting all your conscious thought onto what fills it!

NOW you are seeing beauty.

What effect does that have on your mood?

Resources

Photography therapy is now a recognized therapy, but it is not practiced very widely. There are many books about the practice, but Jan Phillips wrote the most practical one I've found: God Is At Eye Level: Photography as a Healing Art. The book has no religious dimension, for those who are wondering; it's just a great example of what you can achieve when you really look at the world.

Of course, photography is simply a technique that works and you don't have to follow my lead on this one. You may find it just as easy to go to the park and look around you. BUT please don't underestimate the power of this technique. Seeing beauty is the most powerful, practical technique that you can use. It has no cost, involves no effort and very little time, and leads to a permanent lifting of the spirits and improvements in your enjoyment of life. A great stress reliever!

We all do it – we all ignore beauty, miss it or render it insignificant in our lives – but it's there waiting for you to interact with it, so why waste that opportunity?

It is stress busting in its purest form… now go hug that tree!

Foundations for stress-free living

- ⦿ Get out into nature as often as possible: visit the beach, woodland, the mountains, or wherever beauty is for you.

- ⦿ When you're walking – whether it's on the school run or to the office – slow down and take in the natural environment, even if it's just an urban landscape, and look for beauty in the people and places you see.

- ⦿ During your working day, take regular breaks to look out of the window, and get out in the fresh air during your lunch break.

- ⦿ If the sun is shining, soak up the rays for 20 minutes – this will also replenish your vitamin D levels and have a very positive effect on your mood.

- ⦿ Bring beauty into your home with fresh flowers, photographs of landscapes that inspire you and, if you have a

suitable area at home, then also create an outside living
space where you can retreat and breathe in the fresh air.

 # Day 27

POSTURE

Most people neglect correct posture, and on the whole never experience any negative effects until quite late in life, backache and neck pain being the most common symptoms.

If a person with high anxiety or stress also suffers with incorrect posture, this can have a profound effect on the intensity of their anxiety symptoms.

On Day 6 (see pages 49–53) I talked about how breathing is one of the most important factors in the Holy Grail of anxiety and stress disorders. If you correct breathing patterns, anxiety levels will fall as a result. It's not the CURE, but it is an enormous help!

Posture has a profound effect on breathing; if muscles and bones are compressed a certain amount of internal restriction has to be expected.

Body language

Anxiety and depression can cause a person to become guarded; they feel subconsciously that they need to protect themselves from danger. Like a scared hedgehog that rolls itself into a ball to protect its soft, vulnerable belly, we too tend to sit with our arms crossed, our legs tucked tightly to our bodies, and our shoulders and torso rolled at the waist when we're anxious or depressed.

This posture is achieved totally subconsciously, but it is seriously unhealthy; it compresses internal organs, including the heart and lungs, and inhibits good circulation. It also causes muscle, tendon, and nerve pain.

If you feel that you are doing this, try to correct it by straightening your back and shoulders. This allows the chest to expand and the lungs and internal organs to relax.

The more you are aware of how you are standing and sitting, the more you can practice good posture. If necessary, ask your relatives, colleagues, and friends to tell you when you are doing it. If you change this, you will feel better almost immediately.

In modern life we are less likely to stand, walk, and run for long periods. Over the last 100 years human habits have evolved quicker than at any other time in history; we have more stressors; life is faster, more expensive, and definitely more competitive. Our bodies, however, have not evolved to accommodate these changes in life practice, and this can cause incompatibility between physiological makeup and activities. Over sustained periods of physical and mental pressure caused by these incompatibilities, physical problems can develop, that manifest as stress.

Physical activity promotes more effective circulation, muscle fitness, cardiovascular fitness, and healthier lungs. Lack of exercise, bad posture, and poor air quality, which is often found in modern offices, can be very damaging. The average office worker probably sits for at least five to six hours of the working day, and only moves to walk to the coffee machine, grabbing a quick cup of stimulant just to kick-start that adrenalin.

Sitting in an office chair is not bad, but it should only be done for short periods, with activity in between. This is because the sitting position compresses the torso and the organs below the diaphragm are pushed upward toward the chest cavity, restricting the lungs and heart. If you're overweight, this compounds the problem. Shorter, shallower breaths are taken, and blood oxygen and blood carbon dioxide levels are compromised.

Work-related stress

Sitting for long periods, and poor breathing and posture could explain many of the symptoms associated with work-related stress. It doesn't take too long for a person's natural breathing patterns to be altered enough to cause some unpleasant symptoms, including anxiety, panic disorders, or depression.

Couple incorrect posture with radiation from monitor screens, poor-quality, recycled air or air conditioning, lack of fresh air, central heating, coffee drinking, long hours, and a demanding workload and it is easy to see why the epidemic of 'work stress' related illness is developing.

To improve your posture, it is important to find a seat that keeps your back straight, and try not to lean onto the desk. In this position the chest cavity is at its optimum size while sitting. Most of my work is done seated at my computer and I used to feel terrible if I'd been seated for long periods. The discomfort was not always apparent immediately, but would sometimes carry over to the next day, showing that breathing can be altered drastically and persistently over extended periods. To combat this I bought a kneeling chair, which has greatly improved my posture.

Physical activity helps to maintain good circulation and allows the skeleton, muscles, and other body tissues to stretch – opening up the joints and allowing the body to breathe. Try to avoid drinking too much coffee or tea, as they are both stimulants. And if you can't resist, then lessen the effect by drinking a glass of water every time you have a cup of coffee or tea.

In addition, make sure you get copious amounts of good quality, fresh air: open a window if you can and try to get outside the building during break times if possible. If you feel that you are suffering from stress at work due to excess workloads, you must talk to your boss or union, if you belong to one; otherwise speak to your medical practitioner about a referral to a stress-management counselor. Do not allow yourself to become ill because of your workload; having time off work because of stress should not be an option. You should not be in a position to be subjected to inappropriate stress and workloads; if you are, talk to someone about it.

Pilates

Excess tension in your body can cause a variety of unpleasant symptoms, including backache, a sore neck and shoulders, carpal tunnel syndrome, lethargy, sleeplessness, resistance to stress, etc.

We are all affected by our posture, but there are techniques to improve posture, breathing, balance, and coordination, and

Pilates is the method that we recommend to redress incorrect breathing, posture, and movement. Learning the postures (and exercises) teaches you to use your core muscles as opposed to more superficial strength muscles to maintain correct alignment, and to enable you to feel stronger and more stable in everything you do.

Pilates is not a treatment, but rather a re-education of the mind and body. Pilates can also help you to redress imbalance in your body by releasing unnecessary tension. It can be applied when you are sitting, lying down, standing, walking, lifting, and other daily activities.

Resources

At our residential Anxiety Recovery retreats and workshops we run Pilates and postural-alignment classes because we understand and recommend their positive benefits. At the retreats we often see dramatic changes in the way that clients feel as their posture improves over the days they attend. Feeling physically balanced is a vital part of anxiety recovery. People of all ages and lifestyles have used Pilates to improve the quality of their lives, and classes are widely available. If you haven't got time to attend a class the techniques can easily be learned from a DVD or a book. Try The Complete Classic Pilates Method *DVD by Miranda Bass. The 34 exercises are presented in easy terms, with warnings and detailed advice on the timing of the breath that is so crucial to the core stability Pilates creates. The exercises culminate in workout programs to maintain and challenge your level of fitness. You can buy this DVD and other resources on Pilates from my online store at www.karmamind.com.*

Foundations for stress-free living

◉ Become conscious of how you are standing and sitting: maintain a straight spine, as this will enable you to take good breaths into your belly. Be particularly conscious of your posture during times that are potentially stressful: e.g. a meeting with your boss or with people that are confrontational. Keeping an open, relaxed posture sends a signal that 'all is well' to the other person and, more importantly, your brain, and this will help you to stay calm and composed.

◉ If you sit for long periods, make sure you take a five-minute break every hour and, if possible, walk around or do some Pilates – you can practice these exercises without leaving your desk or attracting unwanted attention. Regularly lift your eyes from your work or computer and focus on the furthest point possible (out of a window for example). This stretches your eyes, but also makes you consciously straighten your neck and back.

◉ If you haven't already, make sure you assess your work–home balance to ensure that work isn't overtaking your life and your health. If it is, take action to redress the balance. See also Day 15 (pages 105–110).

◉ Make sure your working environment is as conducive as possible: make sure your chair is adjustable and has armrests and back support; and get a foot support if you need one; your monitor or equipment is at the right height for you to work comfortably and without back or neck strain. Ensure your workspace is well lit and at a comfortable temperature. If your environment is too dark, too noisy, too hot or too cold this will negatively affect your posture and could be a source of physical stress.

⊙ This is more applicable to women than to men, but wearing high-heeled shoes for extended periods can affect your posture and wellbeing. Everyone should wear well fitting, comfortable shoes, particularly if they have to stand for long periods: for example, at a counter or a workbench. Badly fitting or uncomfortable shoes can cause leg and back pain, and so negatively affect your posture.

 # Day 28

MASSAGE – THE BEST THERAPY

I cannot overstate how important and beneficial massage can be in the treatment of stress-related tension and muscle pain, in mental release of tension and stress, and for general wellbeing.

The benefits of a full-body massage (lasting about 40 minutes) with a trained and experienced masseur (the local holistic health center can be a good place to find a practitioner) are incredible, and include:

⊙ Pain relief

⊙ Reduced anxiety and clinical depression

⊙ Improved circulation (massage temporarily reduces blood pressure and heart rate)

⊙ Stimulates the release of endorphins and serotonin (the body's feel-good hormones)

⊙ Improved scar tissue

⊙ Optimizing the function of the lymphatic system

⊙ Improved sleep

◉ Removes muscle tension and assists in rehabilitation of soft tissue injuries.

If you suffer with psychological or physical stress, a full-body massage with or without aromatherapy oils is fantastic. It is extremely relaxing and softens up all of those tight sinews and muscles. In addition, a head massage is a quick fix and can have an amazingly positive effect on how you feel.

In addition to the benefits that can be achieved by having a regular full-body massage, there are a number of alternative massages therapies available. The ones listed below are those that we have found to be the most helpful in relieving stress.

Hot stone massage

The benefits are not as great as with a conventional full-body massage, but this feels great and is highly recommended.

Reflexology

Unless you fly through the roof when you have your feet tickled, reflexology is very relaxing and certainly seems to have a therapeutic effect. It claims to manipulate organs around the body through the soles of your feet. Sounds far-fetched I know, but I've experienced a number of occasions when an ailment has been detected by a reflexologist practitioner massaging my feet. Reflexology is a great stress reliever and doesn't tickle at all. You can have the practitioner do light touch reflexology or a firmer approach.

Indian head massage

I can't say enough about this practice. If you have never had one, try it! Ask the therapist to massage your face and forehead, too; it's amazing for migraine, neck pain, or that 'stuffy head' feeling, and great for clearing the sinuses. You can have it done with or without smelly oils.

Stress-busting distress

If you suffer from stress symptoms, tension, and anxiety, here is my timetable for minimizing their effects:

- ◉ Once a week: Get a full back, neck, and shoulders massage by a pro or by a partner… it doesn't matter which. With hands or using a handheld massager.

- ◉ Twice a week minimum: Indian head massage by pro or partner.

- ◉ As a treat: Full-body aromatherapy massage once or twice a month.

- ◉ Once every two weeks: Reflexology with a pro, although the techniques can be learned and done by yourself or a partner.

Resources

If you can't afford to get a regular massage from a professional, then get your partner to do it for you. Massage isn't difficult to learn to do at home, and you can even do it to yourself.

You can also purchase massager tools, and I would recommend the Acumag all-over massager. I first tried this machine at a health and beauty show in London. I have tried many massage machines in my time but this one really hit the spot! I didn't hesitate to buy it. I also tried an eye massager – which can be worn backwards to massage the back of the head – and my eyes, tired from three days of non-stop work, felt refreshed, so I bought one of those, too! These are both powerful and versatile massage tools; you can just apply more pressure if you need a firmer touch.

If you would like to try these machines for yourself, read up on massage techniques, or perhaps arm yourself with the basics. Visit www.karmamind.com.

Foundations for stress-free living

◉ A massage can be as simple as spending extra time massaging your scalp when you wash your hair or rubbing in some skin lotion or massage oil after your shower or bath (and yes, they make skin lotions for men, too). The basics are to use firm strokes and work upward toward the heart.

◉ If you have a partner, spend time massaging each other's neck, shoulders, back, legs, and feet. You never know, it might be the start of increased intimacy, and a healthy sex life is one of the most powerful stress-busting tools out there.

◉ Your skin is your biggest organ and it deserves some tender loving care. Drinking plenty of clear fluids throughout the day (e.g. water) is the best way to keep your skin hydrated and help flush out toxins (via your sweat glands).

◉ Aromatherapy oils are reputed to have a wide range of benefits, and can enhance mental and physical wellbeing when used in combination with massage. Sniff out some blends that appeal and use them regularly to help you relax and wind down.

# Day 29

HOBBIES AND FUN

Do you have a hobby? Do you have fun?

Why don't kids get stressed? Because they have too much fun!

They laugh, they joke, they take very little seriously, and they are, on the whole, blissfully unaware of the complexities and frailty of life.

Adults, on the other hand, know all too well about the complexities and frailty of life, don't we? Bills, loans, jobs, kids, commitments... it's surprising really that we remain sane at all.

I have many friends (lucky me), and they fall into two categories: those who have fun and those who don't! Take my friend Matt. He might let his guard down and chuckle out loud occasionally, but, most of the time, he sits there quietly sipping his drink. Does he have a hobby? NO! Does he go anywhere without his family? No. Does he tinker in a potting shed? No!

You see Matt, like many men and women I know, is a plodder. He's a survivor and simply goes through the motions of life – solving problems as they arise, never challenging himself, or anyone else for that matter, always towing the line.

Now you see, I don't tow the line... and I don't think you should either. Instead, aim to be one of the people who manufacture the line and rent it out to everyone else. Then, like me, you'll have fun and when people are with you, they'll have fun too. I know this because it wasn't always like that for me. In fact, when I was younger, I was always the designated driver, the guy holding the ladies' coats as they danced with my friends in the disco; I was 'the sensible one.' I had fun... sort of! But nothing like the fun I have now.

These days I tinker with my old Austin car, I take photographs, I love motor racing so I go to race days and race myself on track days, I walk up BIG hills, I'm an activist, I socialize, and I HAVE FUN!

Do you?

If not, WHY NOT?

Bring in some interest and fun

When you say the word hobby to most people, model trains, knitting, and golf spring to mind. Most people switch off to the concept because it seems like something that men in their 70s do when they retire. Hobbies are actually any activity done outside of the work environment that gives you a sense of wellbeing and fulfillment, or acts as a simple diversion from the pressures of life.

Everyone needs a release. A place where they can go to do or not do anything they wish. A POTTING SHED – metaphorically speaking of course.

Women can have potting sheds, too, although they may call theirs yoga classes, pottery, life drawing classes, photography classes, etc. Same deal, just a lot more sensible and intelligent than what most of us men do!

So, if you haven't got a potting shed... find one! I guarantee that by just taking that little bit of time to do what makes you happy for a few hours every week, your stress levels will reduce and your sense of wellbeing, and your conversational skills, will increase quickly.

If you already have your potting shed, just check that you haven't built it on top of anyone else's, because selfishness is a relationship exterminator!

CASE HISTORY *Gladys, aged 77, homemaker*

We welcomed a wonderful lady called Gladys to one of our retreats. Gladys had high anxiety and panic attacks. At the age of 17 Gladys had married, and since then she had never realized her dreams. She had left school, married, had children, and then waited for her husband to retire. Her main role was to look after the house, and watch her husband as he went around and around the lawn on his tractor-mower. All her life she had knitted, made clothes for her family, and altered clothes for friends and relatives. She loved fashion and fabrics, and had she had the opportunity when she left school, she would have become a fashion designer. Her hobby had become an obsession, but her husband was intolerant and she had slowed down in order to watch him on his mower from the bench in her garden, which is how he liked it.

Having been through the retreat program, Gladys learned to prioritize – to create structure in her day, and to separate family time from her own time. She learned to integrate her hobby and passion into her day, and shortly afterward enrolled on a fashion design degree course at her local university. Gladys has finally realized her dream and she now wakes every day excited by her projects. Her husband is coming to terms with her creative outlet.

Finding a hobby

The best way to find your hobby is to start thinking about what you 'used' to love doing. You know, before all the seriousness of being an adult got in the way. Perhaps you loved puzzles or crafts, fishing with your dad, playing chess, learning foreign languages, or playing the piano or in a band. Perhaps you rode a motorbike but exchanged it for four wheels when the kids came along. How about long walks or rides in the countryside, or playing sports, horse riding, mountain climbing, creative writing, or rollerblading. Think about the things you used to love doing and then do them.

The thing is, I can't find a hobby for you, only you can do that. But hobbies are my lifeline, so all I can say is, go for it!

Remember: time and resources are important

Just make sure that whatever hobbies or activities you choose to take up, you have sufficient time and resources to support them easily. Your hobbies and interests don't have to be time consuming, or require lots of equipment; they just need to give you some regular doses of fun. They might be as simple as borrowing some camping equipment and spending a couple of nights in a local campsite enjoying living out in the wild.

Foundations for stress-free living

⊙ Remember all that YOU time that you created on Day 18 (see pages 121–126), well now you know what to do with it. If your time is already restricted, consider a hobby that could include the rest of the family (e.g. walking, cycling, sport, or photography), or one that you could do from the comfort of your home, such as gardening, painting, or crafts.

⊙ If money is an issue and your newfound hobby requires financial investment (e.g. you want to learn to ride a motorbike or return to riding after a few years off the road), then add this 'goal' to the priority list you made on Day 17 (see pages 117–120) and in the meantime start researching your hobby and treat yourself occasionally to the next best thing: e.g. renting a bike for the weekend or a day out at the races.

⊙ You don't have to have just one hobby either: play with a few ideas and just see what sparks your interest.

⊙ If you're one of the lucky ones, you might even find that your newfound hobby inspires such a passion in you that you begin to realize you could earn your living from what you love doing.

 # Day 30

LOOK AND FEEL GREAT!

Look in the mirror. What do you see? How do you feel about you? Do you like what you see? Does what you see make you feel a certain way?

If, like most of the billions of humans who walk the Earth, you are self-critical, if you are affected by the way you look, if you mention things you would like to change about yourself in conversation and wince when you look in the mirror, then perhaps it's time you took the bull by the horns and did something about it.

Small steps every day bring big changes

Eating well and getting the right levels of vitamins and minerals should now be having a positive effect on your mental and physical health, as well as how you look and feel. If you haven't noticed any positive changes, ask yourself:

◉ How is your healthy eating plan going? If you've given up sugar and stimulants, and are filling your body with nourishment then over time it will help you to lose those extra pounds and feel better.

◉ Are you getting the right amount of sleep each day? Lack of sleep can really take a toll on your self-esteem, making it more difficult to enjoy each day. It can also result in dark circles around your eyes and listless skin.

◉ Are you exercising every day? Low-impact exercises such as tai chi, yoga, and Pilates aren't designed to help you lose weight, but they will strengthen and tone your body.

◉ Are you getting out in the fresh air, making time for 'you' and the hobbies you enjoy? Enjoying yourself and having fun makes you feel good, which in turn makes you feel better about being you. Beauty comes from within, but it starts by doing the activities and being with the people that make you smile.

◉ Are you using the visualizations on the CD to help you feel more relaxed, empowered, and confident?

Use the ideas you've learned over the last 30 days to make a positive difference to how you look and feel.

Reward yourself with a makeover

You've worked hard to offload your stress, so maybe it's time to reward yourself by taking care of your appearance. Ask yourself the following questions:

◉ When was the last time you had a haircut or color. Are you going gray? Does your hair color work for you?

- ⊙ Do your clothes reflect your age and fit you correctly?

- ⊙ Is your eyewear up to date and does it suit your face?

- ⊙ Do you need to work a bit harder at losing weight?

- ⊙ Is your lifestyle (lack of sleep, exercise, drinking, smoking, etc.) taking a toll on your appearance?

There are a million questions I could ask you that could identify what you are doing now that you could change today, to make you feel MUCH better about yourself immediately!

Most stores have personal shoppers, advisors, and stylists etc., so USE THEM. Have your hair done, go and get a free makeover at your local department store… the cosmetics counters will be glad to ply you with every new product designed for your 'skin type' available. Take advantage and get some advice.

Men, do the same. Feeling fresh and well groomed will have a remarkable effect on your self-esteem. Trust me, just getting a quality hair cut and shave can make you feel so much more positive.

You see, if you don't like what you see in the mirror, you will behave differently – less confidently, less positively. Body image is how you feel about yourself and you probably see yourself very differently to how you are seen by other people.

Work on things that you can do RIGHT NOW to make you feel better about you, and keep using the ideas you've learned over the last 30 days to do the things that may take a little longer.

 Remember: self-love is important, too
I am not suggesting you remortgage the house to pay for cosmetic surgery, that you go on a crash diet, or dye your

hair pink. In fact, it is much more important to love yourself for who and what you are – accepting yourself is vital. However, it is worth taking some time to decide what you could do to make yourself feel better about the reflection you see in the mirror every day.

Foundations for stress-free living

◉ Being overly critical of your appearance and features is not helpful, whereas an honest appraisal of the things you could do to make you look and feel good each day and then doing something about them will make you feel better.

◉ Spend time on your appearance each week: perhaps add in a new beauty regime, polish your shoes, upgrade your eyewear, or treat yourself to a day at a local spa.

◉ Declutter your drawers and closets of all those clothes and items that no longer fit you, never fitted you, or that you haven't worn for years. This will make space for the clothes that do fit and suit you.

◉ Even if you have been with your partner for longer than you can remember, regularly tell them they are attractive and sexy to you; be positive and specific in describing how you feel about them. Over time, it's easy to forget to tell the people closest to us that they are still special and attractive.

◉ Lack of rest can make you look and feel lackluster and miserable. Getting the right amount of sleep every night will keep your eyes bright and sparkling, your skin smooth and clear, and your energy levels high. See also Day 9 (pages 69–74).

STRESS FREE EVER AFTER

Okay, if you've reached this part of the program and still feel stressed, it's probably because you haven't bothered to implement the advice, or there is something you've missed.

Ask yourself whether you're making use of the program's vital ingredients by:

⊙ Creating physical equilibrium through the tips I've recommended throughout this book – diet, posture, and breathing, for example.

⊙ Ensuring that you have organized an appropriate work/life balance and timetabled YOU time for time alone and being with your loved ones.

⊙ Creating structure in all that you do to avoid confusion and conflict. Use a diary if necessary.

⊙ Making sure you do all you can to look and feel your best.

⊙ I am not saying that you can cure all of your stress overnight – you probably won't – but if you implement the advice contained in this book, you will be taking long and positive steps toward significantly reducing your stress and anxiety in the short term and developing the positive habits and changes in your perception of your world to achieve long-term success.

Don't be a slave to your perception of your world. Bring structure to your thoughts, love and happiness to your life, and fulfillment to each and every moment you live.

You need money to live, that's a fact, but you don't have to be a slave to the environment in which you live. You have the ability and right to modify your environment, to focus on the positives, to ignore or expel the negatives, and to become a more fulfilled and happier person.

This is your life: as far as we know, we only get one… make it count, starting RIGHT NOW!

RESOURCES

The Linden Method

For more information, resources, and support, visit Charles Linden's website: www.charles-linden.com

For Linden Anxiety Recovery Retreats and Workshops, visit www.anxietyrecoveryretreat.com

The following useful books, CDs, and DVDs are available from www.thelindenmethod.com

The Linden Method Program (printed and digital versions) ISBN: 978-0954980306

The Linden Method Junior Edition Program (ages 7–17) ISBN: 978-0954980313

The Linden Method Program with The Linden Method Workshop 3-DVD set

Stress Free in 30 Days 2-DVD set ISBN: 978-1-78180-183-3

Other titles by Charles Linden

The Linden Method for Anxiety, Panic Attacks, Phobias and OCD; ISBN: 0-9549-8030-1

For *The Linden Method* app for iPhone, iPad, and iPod visit: www.thelindenmethodmobile.com

Other recommended resources

101 Power Thoughts (CD) Louise L. Hay (Hay House, 2004) ISBN: 978-1-4019-0396-1

Self-Esteem Affirmations (CD), Louise L. Hay (Hay House, 2006) ISBN: 978-1-5617-0532-0

The Shift (DVD), Dr. Wayne W. Dyer (Hay House, 2009) ISBN: 978-1-4019-2634-2

The Story of I Can't, Robert Holcroft Page with Julie Fisher (Turtle Dreams, 2006); ISBN 978-0-9554-2050-4

NOTES

ABOUT THE AUTHOR

www.jamiehughesphotography.com

Charles Linden suffered from high anxiety, panic attacks, agoraphobia, and OCD, which severely limited his enjoyment of life until he was 27 years of age. During a particularly severe bout of anxiety, during which he was taking antidepressants, addicted to tranquilizers, and having weekly CBT sessions and psychotherapy, Charles decided that enough was enough. He researched and developed a process that changed his life in days, with permanent results, and has since then helped tens of thousands of anxious people from around the world to find freedom from anxiety disorders.

Charles's program, The Linden Method, and the resultant distance learning, residential and home learning programs he developed, are respected, recommended, and referred to by ex-clients, medics, psychologists, and health care facilities from every corner of the world.

Charles is an adviser to government bodies, the media, and numerous other organizations, and regularly appears on international TV and radio, and in international magazines and newspapers. Charles's clients range from Australian ranchers to aristocracy, Hollywood film stars, and clergymen.

The Linden Method programs are referred to as a new branch of psychological practice, and Charles continues to develop new methods, programs, and formats to enable sufferers of stress and anxiety to navigate the fastest route to freedom from their conditions and symptoms.

www.lindenmethodanxietyrecovery.com